Airfix Model W
Basic Gui
Modelli...g

STU FONE

KEY
Books

Contents page image: Regardless of whether paint is brushed or sprayed, its recommended that multiple light layers are used, rather than a single heavy one – as seen here on Airfix's 1/72 Jet Provost T.3/4.

Published by Key Books
An imprint of Key Publishing Ltd
PO Box 100
Stamford
Lincs PE19 1XQ

www.keypublishing.com

This book is a collection of articles orginally published as the Back to Basics series in *Airfix Model World* magazine © Key Publishing Ltd.

ISBN 978 1 80282 208 3

Typeset by SJmagic DESIGN SERVICES, India.

Contents

Chapter 1

Tools of the Trade

Here is a very basic toolkit, with glue, thinners, paint, tweezers, craft knives, scissors, a sanding stick and files, plus brushes, all on a small cutting mat.

For those entering the hobby for the first time, welcome. For those returning, welcome back. Modelling is one of the most relaxing and satisfying pastimes, offering a wealth of creative opportunities and years of enjoyment. The aim of this book is to provide an elementary grounding in the tools and techniques required, on which readers can then build their skills.

For this introduction, we'll look at what makes a 'core' toolkit for building your first few kits, although exactly what goes into your own version is completely up to you.

Where to start

In its simplest form, modelling equipment can be reduced to a means of cutting parts from runners, handling the individual components (especially those smaller items), gluing them together, painting them and adding decals. The great news is all such tools are readily available at local craft/hobby shops at minimal cost – ideal for those new to modelling. A small sub-set of equipment helps to make the aforementioned easier (such as a cutting mat and steel ruler), so an initial shopping list could look like this:

- Craft knife
- Side-action cutters
- Cutting mat
- Scissors
- Holding aids (including tweezers, clothes pegs or clamps, cocktail sticks, tape)
- Glue
- Sanding paper/pads/sticks
- Files
- Paintbrushes
- Paint
- Steel ruler

Cutting tools

Craft knives are the usual method of removing parts from runners and there is a broad range of styles, from slide-action types with blade sections that can be snapped off when the edges become blunt, to handles with interchangeable blades. Among the latter are the American-made X-Acto series and British Swann Morton scalpels, and there is a wide range of straight and curved edged blades that can be fitted. Note that the blades are very sharp and best not used by children, even with adult supervision; X-Acto's blades are stronger, but Swann Morton's are sharper. Side-action cutters, comprising two angled blades that are brought together in a scissor-style action, have the advantage of being more robust than knife blades and are easier for younger modellers to use. Fine scissors are also invaluable, whether it's for cutting decals from the surrounding sheet or trimming tape for masking.

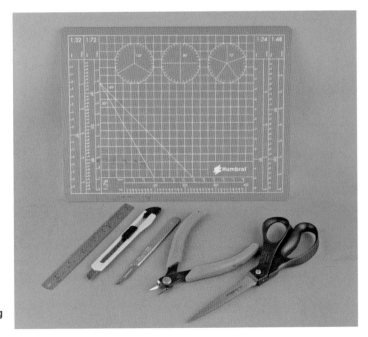

Cutting tools come in various forms, from craft knives to 'snippers' and scissors, while aids such as a steel rule ensures straight lines and cutting mats protect underlying surfaces.

Outside of these key items, a cutting mat is a must, as it protects any underlying surfaces from damage while also acting as a handy modelling 'desk'. Several firms, such as Humbrol, produce bespoke modelling workstations, incorporating a cutting mat on a plastic base, with integral holders for paints, brushes and glue. A steel ruler (flexible if possible) is also well worth the initial expense, as it's hard wearing and resistant to damage and can be used when cutting flat parts or masking tape, scratch-building or re-scribing (see page 11 and Chapter 11).

Getting a grip

Once items have been removed from runners, there's often a need to handle them while they are painted and/or assembled, especially if they're small. Tweezers are very useful and are available in

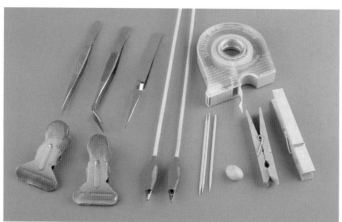

Not all tools have to come from a hobby shop. These tweezers and bulldog and crocodile clips were sourced from a stationary and automotive store, while everything else is available from most supermarkets and craft shops.

packs offering pointed, angled, reverse-action (squeeze to open) and flat-bladed forms. Small crocodile clips are handy tools when it comes to painting small parts, along with bulldog clips or clothes pegs for larger pieces. Similarly, masking or common household tape is great for holding items together when dry-fitting, but can also assist when removing small parts from the runner, as can Blu Tack. Simply loop the tape adhesive side outward and stick it to your workbench, press the part against it and, when it's separated from the frame, it won't be catapulted off the desk in the dreaded 'ping' moment. Cocktail sticks are ideal when painting wheels, as they can be inserted into axle holes, and can be used with tape or Blu Tack on tiny components.

Stuck together

Styrene adhesives generally work by softening the mating surfaces to a greater or lesser degree, after which pressure serves to 'weld' the parts together. They are usually produced in tubes or bottles – the former has a thick, almost jam-like consistency, while the latter is liquid and comes with an applicator brush. The basic rule-of-thumb is that the thinner the solution, the quicker the drying time.

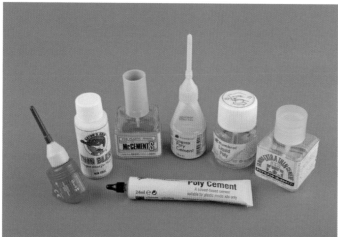

There is a surprising variety of adhesives on the market, but most are liquids and dispensed via a dropper needle or brush, while tube glue is still used (often in starter sets). White glue (also known as wood glue or PVA) dries clear and can be cleaned with water when wet, making it ideal for transparent parts, such as canopies.

Adding colour

It wasn't too long ago that there were just four major paint manufacturers, three of which (Humbrol, Revell and Testors) produced oil-based enamels, while the fourth (Tamiya) favoured an alcohol-based acrylic formula. There are now approximately 20 firms producing shades in lacquer, alcohol-based acrylic, water-based acrylic and enamel compositions (listed in order of drying time from fastest to slowest). Novice modellers may find enamels the easiest to start with as they take longer to dry, but water-based acrylics are increasingly popular with beginners and often feature in 'starter' or 'gift' sets (see photo), along with glue and brushes.

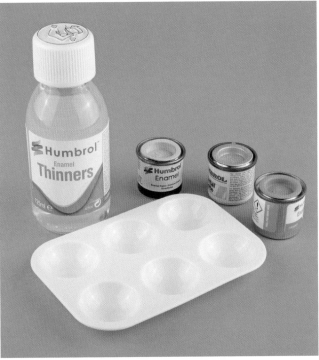

Thinners are required for cleaning brushes and diluting the colours for brush/airbrush application, although there are now 'airbrush-ready' products, which have a less viscous consistency. Most paint manufacturers produce their own thinners, and some can work with other brands, but use of the firm's own products is recommended until your level of experience grows.

A mixing/blending palette is a very useful piece of equipment, either for diluting paints or mixing bespoke colours. These are very cheap to buy and are made from a hard-wearing plastic or ceramic that tolerates even the harshest lacquer and/or thinners formulations.

Above: Basic elements for painting are the colours, proprietary thinners and a mixing palette (either for diluting or blending).

Below: There are four main types of modelling paint, from left to right: lacquers, alcohol-based acrylics, water-based acrylics and enamels – each of which requires a different type of thinners.

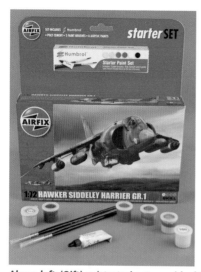

Above left: **'Gift' or 'starter' sets are ideal for a first kit, as they provide all necessary paints, plus brushes and adhesive a modeller will need for a basic build.**

Above right: **You'll need various sizes of paint brushes, with rounded (for fine items and detail) and flat (for area coverage) shaped versions. Starter set items are ideal initially, but always try to buy the best you can afford (ideally sable) and clean them carefully to preserve the bristles.**

Neatening the parts

When it comes to cleaning up components before assembly, abrasive paper (also known as sandpaper) is a vital tool. This can come as paper-type sheets (such Wet and Dry, found at most hobby and automotive stores), combined with a foam 'pad' as a sanding stick (see photos), or imprinted onto a fabric base as a cloth. There are varying grades, with the coarsest having the lowest value

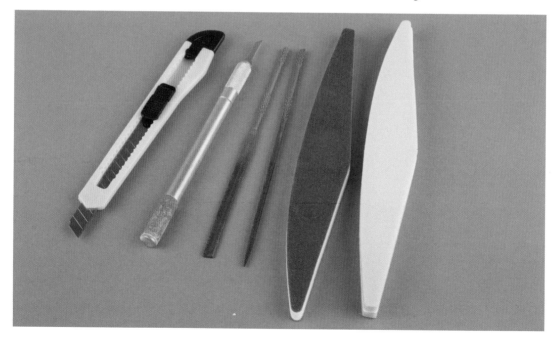

Opposite below: In addition to Wet and Dry abrasive paper sheets, files and foam-padded sanders are ideal for smoothing and neatening parts, while knives can be used as scrapers and sanders by gluing abrasive paper to the handle.

Right: While this build of Hasegawa's 1/700 IJN *Furutaka* is more advanced, it's notable that many items identified in the 'core' shopping list are present; knife, clippers, cocktail sticks, and tweezers.

Here, they have been used for the ship's rigging, but, as will be seen, they have multiple uses.

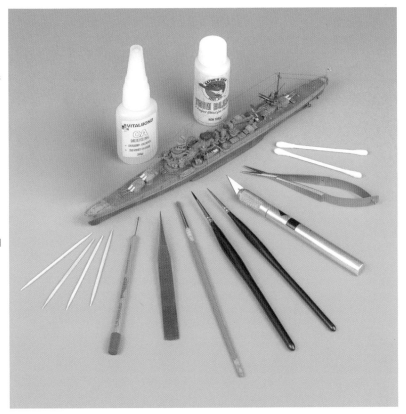

(400-grade sanders are good general-purpose implements, while 1,200-grade are excellent for final smoothing). Small metal files are invaluable for getting into small areas, although these are usually rougher, while craft knives have a dual role – they can be used as scrapers or else abrasive paper can be wrapped around the handle to neaten curved surfaces.

Next steps

As you gain more experience and seek to refine builds by eliminating assembly seams and any blemishes on decals, the following items could be added to your toolkit, depending on personal preferences. We'll cover these later in the book.

- Razor saws (also called craft saws)
- Modelling putty
- Decal setting solutions
- Cyanoacrylate adhesive (CA, known popularly as superglue)
- Fine-grade abrasive/sanding cloths
- Scribing tools
- Weathering products (washes, pigments)
- An airbrush

Chapter 2

The First Cuts

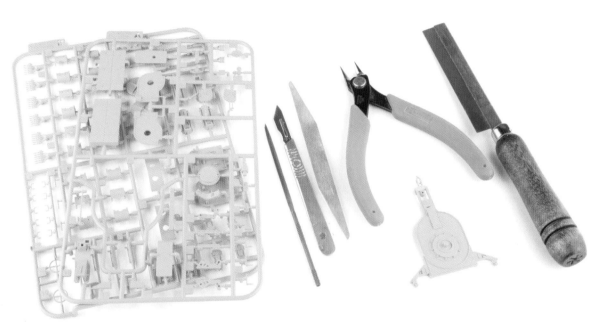

The first tasks in a build are separating the parts from the runner and then removing any remnants of the attachment stub – basic tools to achieve this task include a craft knife, razor saw, snippers, file and sanding pads/paper.

Having got your kit onto the hobby table, the aim of these initial preparatory stages is to make sure everything fits properly – ensuring the joins aren't fouled by any plastic stubs from the attachment points – and to ready the parts for painting.

As with many aspects of the hobby, much of this will be a matter of personal choice, such as the tools used and the quality of the finish, but overall these principles hold true for all modellers. One particular area of discussion concerns whether parts should be washed prior to use – old moulding techniques employed a 'release agent', which often left a residue that had to be removed, otherwise it was difficult to get paint or glue to adhere. This isn't true of more modern offerings, but several types of styrene appear 'greasy' and would benefit from a wash in soapy water before being rinsed. If this 'greasiness' remains, the offending areas can be cleaned with a cotton bud dipped in thinners.

When parts go 'ping'

The first challenge is to remove the components. For this, a craft knife or side-action clippers are ideal. However, a small razor saw may be required for larger attachment gates, as their size may make it difficult to use the other tools. As its name suggests, a razor-saw has a fine-toothed (and very sharp) blade and comes in a variety of sizes; the most common are approximately 4in (10cm) long and with a ½in (12mm) deep cutting blade; these are available from most hobby/craft shops. More specialised saws have one or more toothed edges and feature a smaller blade with finer serrations (usually measured in teeth per inch). However, the process is the same, regardless of how expensive the saw is, using light pressure as the blade is moved back and forth over the surface to be cut.

This brings us onto a common topic, namely how to deal with small pieces. If not handled properly, they can be lost easily (the dreaded 'ping' into the far corners of the hobby room), especially if they fall onto a carpet (also known as the 'monster' for the way it 'eats' parts). There are various ways to address this problem and all involve securing the parts with an adhesive substance, a finger or by enclosing everything in a clear bag (so everything remains visible and it's the plastic – not your fingers – that is cut).

Separating components

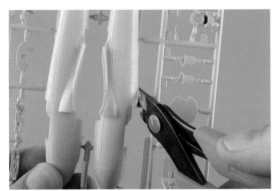

Above left: Clippers are a safe and easy way of removing parts, but care should be taken to ensure the 'flat' face butts against the component, otherwise a larger attachment stub will remain.

Above right: A sharp craft knife can either be pressed onto an attachment gate or drawn across it several times to gradually cut through the styrene, although care must be taken as blades are very sharp.

Right: Razor saws should be saved for the thickest attachment points and, rather than cutting quickly through the styrene, light pressure should be used – this reduces the risk of slippage that could easily damage the part (or your fingers).

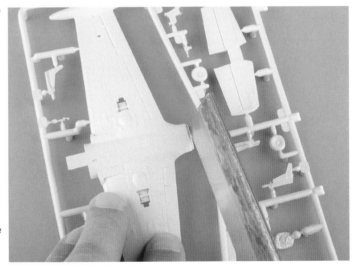

Keeping everything together

If there's one frustrating aspect of model-making, it's when small pieces are lost, either due to over-exuberant cutting or being knocked off the modelling table accidentally. Some of the best methods for retaining parts are also the simplest, such as holding everything with tape or Blu Tack, or conducting the cutting in a transparent bag, so nothing can go astray. Another basic method is to apply light pressure on the object with a finger while cutting – not too much pressure, though, as this can also cause a 'ping' moment!

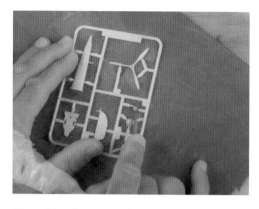

Above left: When using a large clear polythene bag, make sure everything (including the actual cutting mat) is inside, otherwise it will gradually get destroyed over time.

Above right: A blob of Blu Tack can be an ideal parts holder, as it will conform to whatever shape is pressed gently into it.

Right: A length of tape looped with the adhesive side outwards can be used to 'stick' the part before cutting with a knife/cutters/saw.

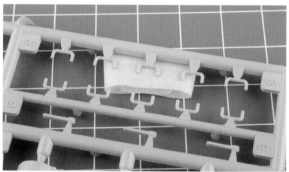

Where to cut

A common dilemma is when delicate parts have two or more runner attachment gates, with the risk of damaging the component depending on the order these are cut. Generally, the best method is to see which of them puts the least strain on the item – if it's surrounded with them, its arguably better to cut at least one with a fine razor saw.

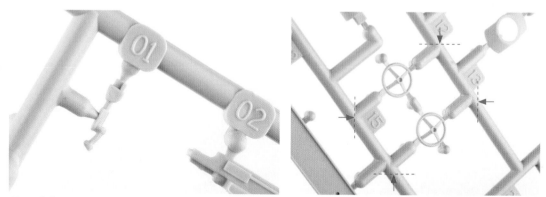

Above left: Here, the control column on Airfix's 1/72 Jet Provost has two runner gates. Ideally, the left-hand one would be the best to cut first, as it doesn't push the part against the other attachment point, which could cause the component to break.

Above right: A more challenging situation is when delicate parts, such as these rotate/elevate handwheels on Dragon's 1/35 Hummel-Wespe, are surrounded by runner gates. Here, the best solution would be to either cut the runner at the positions shown (arrowed) or use a razor saw to cut both upper attachment points – that way, removing any of the other gates won't place any stress or deform the component.

Neatening edges

No matter how careful a modeller is in separating the parts from the runner, there is usually an element of residue, called a stub, which must be removed to ensure the components fit together properly. While most are located on the sides, there is a growing number of companies putting these on the lower surfaces to minimise damage to the kit's exterior detail. Both respond well to initial careful trimming with a sharp knife, followed by sanding.

Another issue that falls in to the 'neatening' category is when there are heavy mould seams and flash (effectively the same thing, but more extensive). Initially, these are best treated with a sharp craft knife to remove most of the excess styrene, followed by either sanding or filing, depending on how small the parts are.

Removing attachment gate burrs

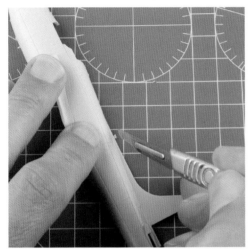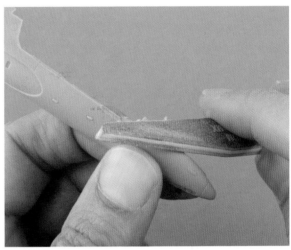

Above left and above right: Any remaining stub can be trimmed easily with a knife and sanded with either abrasive paper or a file.

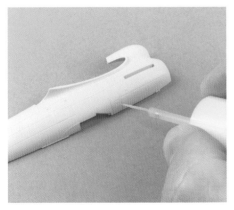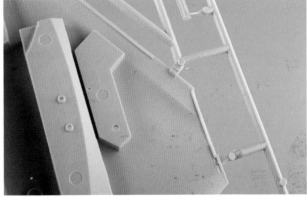

Above left: Last, liquid cement can be brushed onto the trimmed edges to smooth the surface and remove any residual debris.

Above right: While most attachment gates are on the model's exterior surfaces, a growing number of manufacturers are now placing them on the underside, to minimise damage to any delicate detail.

Flash and ejector pin marks

Parts quality – especially in terms of moulding – is usually related to the age of a kit, with older offerings featuring more in the way of heavy seam lines and flash (although several modern releases also suffer from this). Many of the tools used for cutting are applicable here, along with abrasive paper/pads and files. As with general neatening chores, liquid cement is great for tidying any rough edges and or debris, while also smoothing the surface. Ejector pin marks can be frustrating, as occasionally they are located on mating surfaces or in places that are visible on the completed model. They can be treated in the same manner as attachment stubs, although those that form depressions in the surface can be resolved with either modelling putty or even layered masking tape cut to shape.

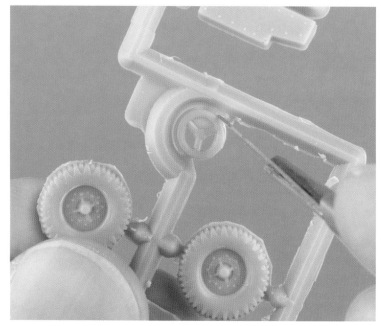

This driver's wheel suffers from flash, which has filled the gap between the part and runner, plus at least one gap between the rim and spokes.

Once the bulk of the flash has been removed with a knife, the surface can then be either scraped to smooth it further, or alternatively treated with a file or abrasive pad/paper.

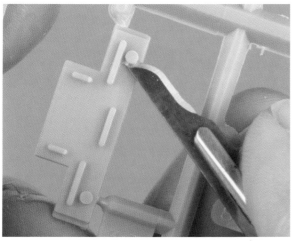 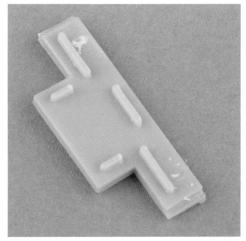

Above left and above right: The rear panel on Airfix's 1/72 Bofors truck has two prominent ejector pin marks (left), which prevent it from attaching correctly to the vehicle's rear equipment box parts, so these must be removed with either a knife or clippers, before being sanded (right).

All those 'bits'

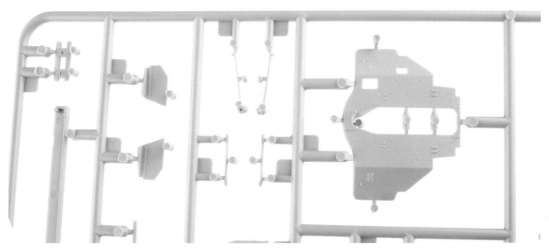

In the past, mould stubs were common on kits by Dragon or Monogram, but have become increasingly prevalent as firms seek to incorporate finer detail into each part. They should be treated in the same manner as attachment gates, by first removing the stub and them trimming/sanding any remaining burrs with a knife and abrasive paper/pad.

Chapter 3

Colour Dilemmas

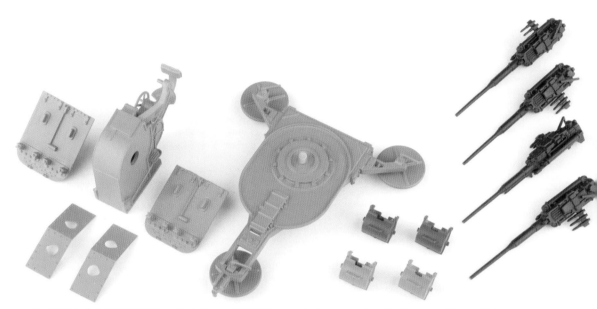

Das Werk's delightful 1/35 3cm Flakvierling 103/38 kit was built as a series of sub-assemblies (which were determined mainly by the colour scheme), rather than following the instruction stages, with the main mount, 30mm cannon, baseplate and gun shields constructed separately before being painted in their initial tones.

It's a rite of passage for modellers new to the hobby (or those returning after an absence) to reach a point where just building a kit isn't enough.

Inevitably, the question of 'when to paint' then raises its head. Unfortunately, there isn't a simple solution, as often it will come down to personal preference or sequencing. There's also the factor that one approach doesn't necessarily work for all genres. Aircraft or car kits, for example, usually require painting of the interior before the fuselage/body is assembled, but many armoured vehicle kits can be almost completely built before you reach for the paint (unless they too have interior detail). Maritime subjects tend to fall somewhere between, especially when there is a complex camouflage scheme or aftermarket photo-etched parts are added.

At the extreme ends of this scale, all components could be painted while still attached to the runners, or else everything could be glued together beforehand. In recent years, there has also been a return to pre-coloured styrene, often combined with 'snap-together' construction, so this type of kit could be built without either paint or glue.

In this chapter, we'll investigate the pros and cons of each of these methods, plus how building in sub-assemblies can help, and we'll introduce the idea of 'scale effect'. This will lead directly into the next chapter, which will explain how to create/accentuate the illusion of depth. Above all, the methods outlined here are for guidance only – as with many aspects of modelling, there is arguably no right or wrong approach – it's more a case of whatever works for you.

Interior parts for Airfix's 1/72 Jet Provost T.3/4 are spread across two runners – the thick runner frame means handling is easy, but care is needed to avoid getting paint on any of the mating surfaces.

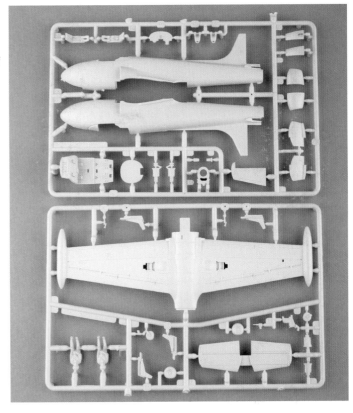

Piece by piece

Whether parts are painted individually or as part of a larger sub-assembly is often decided by the subject. Here, the process is examined using Airfix's 1/72 Jet Provost Mk.3/4 as the main example. First, a decision must be made whether to paint the parts either on the runner or when detached. Each approach has its own advantages/disadvantages – the former is easier to handle, but the latter means there's less need for touch-up work later.

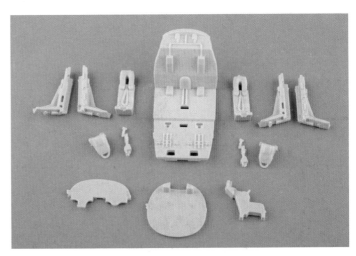

Another approach is to remove all the parts first and then paint them – less neatening is required afterwards, but smaller items (such as the control columns) can be fiddly to handle.

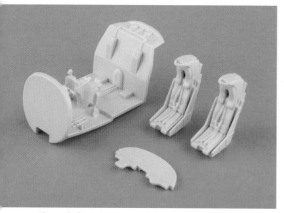

Above left: Sub-assemblies can provide the advantages of both the previously mentioned techniques, as well as minimise the downsides. Here, the cockpit has been split into four sections: 'tub' and bulkheads, two ejection seats and an instrument panel. Often the best way to determine how much can be built into each sub-assembly is to look at which items will receive the same colour, balanced against the ease of actual painting.

Above right: Here, Airfix's basic painting suggestions have been followed for one cockpit (left), which has received Humbrol 85 Coal Black, while that on the right has been treated with a very dark grey tone to provide scale effect. The latter is very much subjective and isn't favoured by all modellers, but it does allow for greater tonal variation when it comes to subsequent shadows/highlights.

All-in-one

An alternative approach is to assemble most of the kit before any painting occurs. While this is common for armoured vehicles with closed hulls, it can also be applied to open-topped subjects with a single-tone camouflage scheme, or where the interior has the same base tone as the exterior, such as staff/utility cars, trucks and self-propelled artillery. Some modellers prefer to complete all construction (even putting tracks on tanks) before reaching for the brush/airbrush – as with many elements of modelling, this is mostly a personal choice.

Often, the way in which the real machinery is painted can determine whether this method is used. The examples shown here should help to illustrate this.

Models depicting 'closed' subjects, such as the Soviet T-34, are ideal for this method of construction, although usually the turret will be kept separate for ease of handling. Airfix's 1/35 offering (a re-boxed Academy kit), which is moulded in dark green styrene, has link-and-length tracks, so even the running gear can be attached if desired, although wheel rims need careful painting.

Airfix's 1/76 Bofors Gun and Tractor is an old but otherwise excellent kit, although the fit is challenging in places. Everything apart from the cab roof (often a different shade, as it was made of canvas) and wheels can be assembled before it needs any paint, as the chassis, body and cargo area are all the same colour.

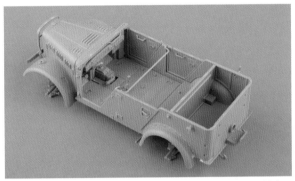

Above left: After a primer coat (used to check for any gaps in joins), the model received Lifecolor's UA269 British Tanks Dark Olive. Certain items, such as the rear stowage boxes, would be hand-painted in different tones later.

Above right: Similarly, most parts of ICM's 1/35 le.gl.Einhetz-Pkw Kfz.1 Soft Top can be assembled before any painting is needed. Here, the main body has been completed in readiness for the German Grey scheme – all it lacks are the wheels, seats (which are a different colour), crew weapons and equipment/tools, plus the soft-top roof.

Halfway house

Sometimes, a build requires the use of both previously described methods – essentially the innards are built/painted as a sub-assembly, then the rest of the model can be completed before applying final camouflage. There are many variations of this basic description, especially when it comes to maritime subjects, as the inclusion of PE extras may require the initial building of the main hull/superstructure in a similar fashion to a tank, followed by external sub-assemblies to accommodate the PE components.

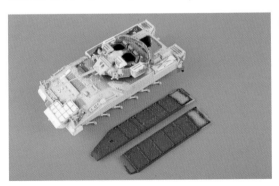

Above left and above right: A similar approach will be required on those military kits with an interior – these could be either open-hulled subjects or offerings with details such as fighting compartments, engines and crew positions. This process also works well when modellers are adding photo-etched metal, resin or scratch-built extras or conversions, with a primer acting to unify the different materials. Here, alterations to Airfix's 1/48 Warrior (backdating it to a Bosnia-deployed machine) are readied for final painting.

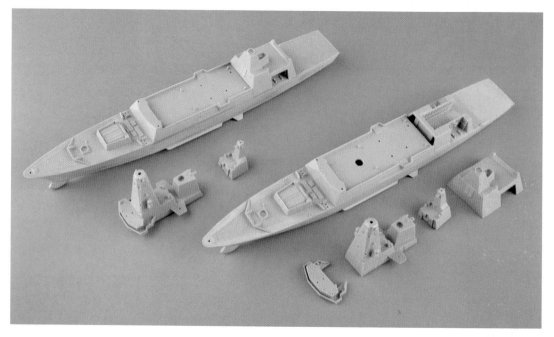

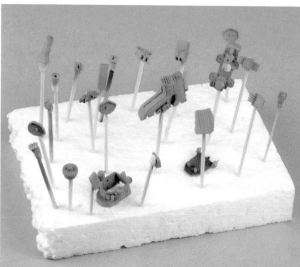

Above: Modern maritime subjects that incorporate signature-reduction measures (also called stealth features) are often 'clean', with enclosed weapons, boats and equipment. As shown with Dragon's 1/700 HMS *Daring*, most parts can be assembled before painting (left) – often, ease of access will dictate how much can be constructed. If open boat-decks and hangar doors are included (right), it's treated as a series of sub-assemblies.

Left: By comparison, older maritime subjects have a more 'cluttered' appearance – especially when PE items are included. This means building a series of sub-assemblies is arguably the best way of approaching construction/painting. Hasegawa's 1/700 *Furutaka* cruiser is a case in point – the superstructure is formed from a series of sub-units, decided after a study of the instructions and the amount of PE being added to each.

Coloured styrene

Some readers may recall Matchbox's range of two- and three-colour kits, which were aimed squarely at beginners, as they could be built without the need for paint. The styrene tones often bore little resemblance to the shades used on the real machines, but it still made for a colourful model. In recent years, at least two companies (Academy and Bandai) have championed this approach, but both strive to match the official hues as closely as possible. Additionally, several manufacturers of wargaming kits have opted for single-colour styrene to match that of a subject where there is an overall camouflage scheme, such as US Federal Standard (FS) 15042 Glossy Sea Blue-painted naval aircraft or FS 34087 Olive Drab tanks.

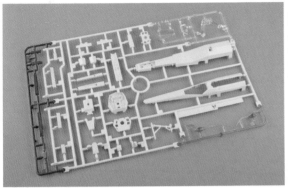

Left: Bandai's range of *Star Wars* kits has raised the bar in terms of styrene colour quality, with clever engineering allowing the firm to present several tones on a single runner. Each shade has been matched carefully with either the studio (the original film trilogy) or CAD models (the prequels and Episodes VII-IX) and enables a model to be built straight from the box without the need for glue or paint. The provision of self-adhesive and waterslide markings makes these kits ideal for modellers of all skill levels.

Right: Similarly, South Korea's Academy has introduced a Multi-Color Plastic (MCP) range, either updating older kits, such as its RMS *Titanic*, or as newly tooled offerings like its 1/72 F/A-18E Super Hornet, F-35A Lightning II and F-4J Phantom. The more recent products can optionally be assembled without glue, so these are great as introductions to the hobby.

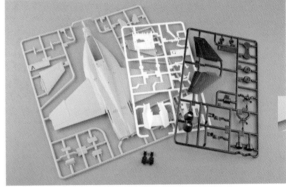

Intended primarily for wargamers, Forces of Valor products are moulded in styrene that's been coloured to match a specific single-tone paint scheme. The aim is to provide an easy-to-assemble kit, and the large locating pins mean these can mostly be built without glue. However, modellers may wish to paint the interior to make it appear more realistic.

Chapter 4

Let There be Light

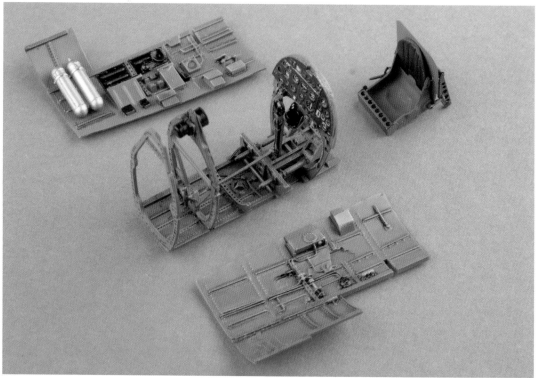

While Airfix's 1/48 Spitfire Mk.I includes a superb cockpit interior, its appearance can be enhanced greatly by using effects that mimic shadows and light.

Whenever you look into a real aircraft or vehicle, those areas furthest from the observer always appear darker, as less light is reflected from those sections. If we look at this from a purely technical aspect, for kits with moulded detail or that use laminated photo-etched parts (such as an instrument panel or interior framework), to build height/depth into an interior, merely painting these areas should be enough. More light will be reflected from the upper areas, but scale then comes into play – often the cockpits/hatches are too small, the colour scheme is monotone or the interior is too shallow for this to become noticeable, so a common modelling technique is to exaggerate these differences. While there are many ways of achieving this, we'll stick to just the basic forms, using a combination of dry-brushing to provide highlights and washes to create shadows.

Where to begin

A good rule of thumb when creating these effects is to work from light to dark. Another is that 'less is more' – it's easier to add small amounts of paint than to remove them if applied too heavily. This chapter will concentrate on Airfix's 1/72 Jet Provost which, as seen in the accompanying photos, has

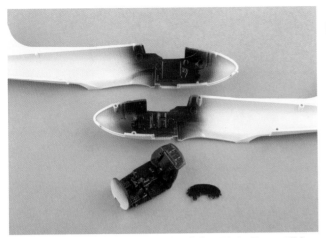

Above and opposite: The cockpit of Airfix's 1/72 Jet Provost T.3 received a protective layer of varnish prior to any highlighting or shadow effects being added.

PROTECTIVE LAYERS

It's important to use a different formula of varnish to the paint and wash to prevent damaging the underlying tones. The accompanying tables offer a handy guide:

Base colour	Varnish
Enamel	Acrylic or lacquer
Lacquer	Acrylic or enamel
Acrylic	Enamel or lacquer
Varnish	Dry-brushing/wash
Enamel	Acrylic or oil
Lacquer	Acrylic, enamel or oil
Acrylic	Enamel or oil

received an acrylic varnish since its appearance in the last issue. This layer is an important addition, as it forms a barrier between the base tones and subsequent work.

A light grey tone was selected for the dry-brushing of the tub and sidewalls (the instrument panel is left alone as this will use the kit decals). Tools required are a stiff or flat brush, some kitchen towel and a degree of patience. The brush is loaded with a small amount of paint, and most of this is then worked onto the kitchen towel, until almost no colour is deposited. It is then brushed lightly against any raised features, concentrating initially on the edges, with the process repeated until the desired effect is achieved. A common issue is getting frustrated with what can be apparently slow progress and applying paint more heavily, the consequences of which can be a very 'blotchy' finish. As you gain more practice in this skill, it's possible to highlight ever smaller features, including instrument bezels and even the buttons for head-down cockpit displays (common in modern jets).

For dry-brushing, all that's needed is a fairly stiff brush, kitchen towel (to remove excess paint), cotton buds, a mixing tray and the desired colour of paint.

Although there are many pre-mixed wash products available, one of the simplest is to use oils and white spirit – these are very cheap in the long run, and can be blended into the underlying colours.

A brush, with almost all paint removed from it, is rubbed gently against the raised surfaces to leave an outline – don't worry if the change appears small, as it's easier to build the effect gradually.

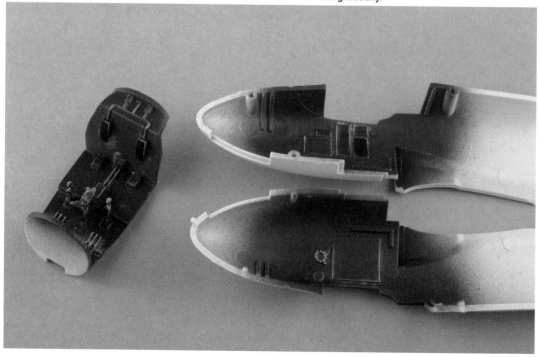

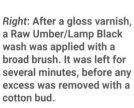

Right: After a gloss varnish, a Raw Umber/Lamp Black wash was applied with a broad brush. It was left for several minutes, before any excess was removed with a cotton bud.

Below: A test-fit of the cockpit tub reveals how the light and dark areas make the moulded features 'pop out', relieving the appearance of what would otherwise be a monotone sub-assembly.

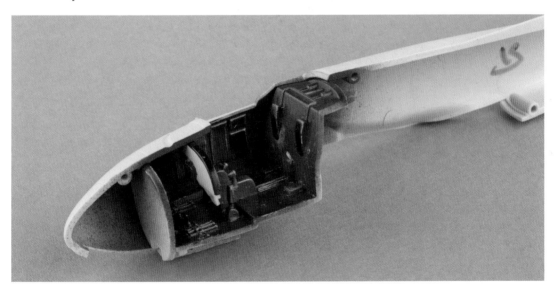

Another benefit of dry-brushing is it can be used to lighten the tone of horizontal surfaces and create a tonal graduation on vertical faces, simulating greater reflection and decreasing exposure to the light source respectively. The latter is a common method used by modellers with airbrushes, but can also be achieved with just a normal hand-held brush.

In the shade

Modellers should note that washes are best applied to gloss surfaces as these help them to 'flow' and 'pool' around features; on matt finishes, a wash will tend to stain the surrounding area. This leads neatly to a common 'gotcha', and that is using the same form of paint/thinners as the underlying

Above: **The principle reason for using these effects is to enhance the appearance of small cockpits (notably if they are dark toned) once the fuselage halves are joined.**

Left: **It's up to the modeller whether to use washes to highlight recessed detail or to open the apertures fully – Airfix's Spitfire frame has the former effect on the left, and latter on the right.**

colours, as these can be damaged by the subsequent applications. Here, with enamels used, the best results were achieved using an acrylic varnish (see *Protective layers*).

Although an oil wash was used in this instance, the basic principles are the same. The colour is mixed to provide a contrast (but not too strong) with the underlying paint, then diluted with thinners. It is then applied with a standard brush and allowed to pool round any raised features. Any excess is removed with a cotton bud, dry brush or kitchen towel. As with dry-brushing, repeated treatments are much better than a single heavy wash – this also allows you to fine-tune the results.

Once satisfied, everything should be set aside to dry thoroughly, after which any touch-up work or replicating the appearance of newly chipped or worn paint can be undertaken, depending upon personal choice.

A matt or satin varnish (depending on the finish used on the real aircraft) then seals all the work to date. As a final touch on Airfix's Jet Provost cockpit, the uppermost boxes/consoles received additional dry-brushing, just to pick out specific elements. The cockpit was then ready for decaling and insertion into the fuselage – once completed (and any other internal sub-assemblies added), the halves can then be closed and glued.

It's not just painting

When kit manufacturers mould components such as bulkheads and structural frames, they often represent lightening holes as just circular depressions. This provides two options for the builder: either

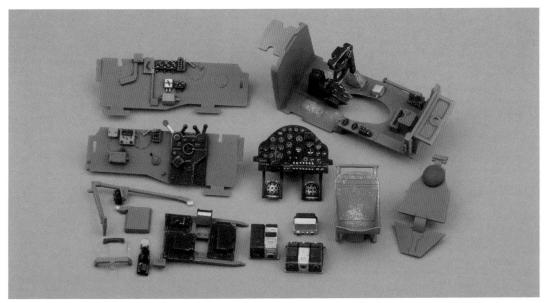

These effects can be used on any cockpit; here the internal components of Tamiya's 1/48 P-38 Lightning have been enhanced with the techniques explained in this chapter.

add a very dark wash to each or else drill them. As seen in the lead photo of Airfix's 1/48 Spitfire Mk.Ia, the interior frames are shown with both methods utilised. A pin vice and associated drills can be bought from most hobby or craft shops, and there is usually at least one trader selling these at model shows, making them a cheap and useful addition to the toolbox.

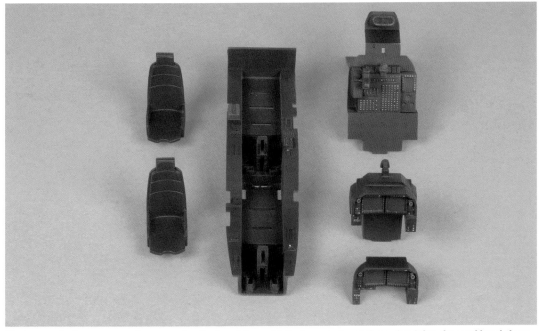

Modern cockpits are a superb canvas for dry-brushing, with their myriad switches, circuit breaker and head-down display buttons all easy to improve with just a little effort.

Chapter 5

Smooth Building

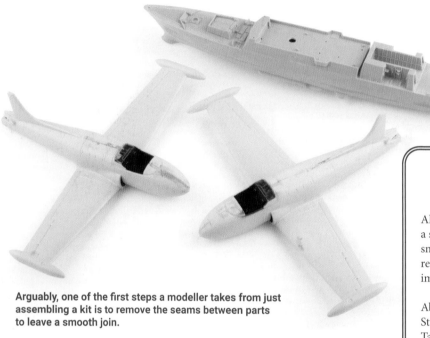

Arguably, one of the first steps a modeller takes from just assembling a kit is to remove the seams between parts to leave a smooth join.

Moulding technology has come a long way in recent years, but there's a common issue facing many modellers: the presence of prominent seams on a model, caused by the parts not fitting together properly.

USEFUL TOOLS

Although outwardly a simple process, smoothing seams can require quite a few implements:

Abrasive paper/pads
Styrene cement
Tape
Grips/clamps/pegs
Steel rule
DYMO tape
Scriber
Razor saw
Spatula

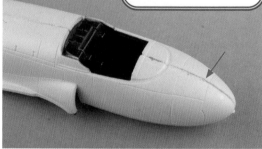

Above left: Keeping the mating surfaces clear of paint is crucial to achieving a good seam – often paint is deposited accidentally (bottom), but a few swipes with a sanding stick can remove it easily (top).

Above right: Older or short-run kits may not be moulded to the same tolerances as mass-produced items, so there may be a 'step' in the styrene, leaving one side higher than the other. Here, the Jet Provost's nose area was twisted slightly in a clamp to help illustrate this issue, as indicated by the arrow.

We will again use Airfix's 1/72 Jet Provost as the 'guinea pig' in this chapter, which will include how to overcome a couple of common errors when treating join lines and surface blemishes.

As with all other aspects for the hobby, preparation is key and begins before the parts are assembled and any glue is applied. It's vital to ensure the mating surfaces are clear of paint – this can interfere with the adhesion, creating a weak join, as well as lead to fitting issues with interior parts as they won't come together correctly. These can be quite a problem with kits developed using CAD software as the tolerances are exceptionally fine – even one or two layers of paint can cause difficulties.

Hopefully, if all goes well when assembling a kit, then any seams will be relatively minor, but the basic process is the same regardless of how severe the problem, although there may need to be repeated treatments to achieve a satisfactory result. While an aircraft is used in this chapter, these methods are applicable to all genres of kit.

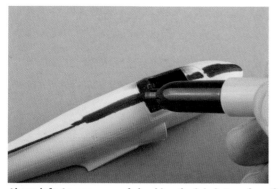 

Above left: An easy way of checking the join is to colour the area with a contrasting tone. Here a permanent marker has been used, but paint (either brushed or airbrushed) is often used – metallic tones are excellent for highlighting blemishes.

Above right: After sanding with a medium-grade abrasive pad, the gaps are revealed. Those on the upper fuselage are minimal, but the 'step' is clearly visible on the lower item. Small marks on either side of the seam were caused by the use of a coarse abrasive pad prior to the marker, showing just how effective this simple method can be at highlighting issues.

Below left: Applying filler/putty can be a messy business, but an easy way to keep everything neat is to use masking tape to set a boundary or 'frame' (bottom). This is then removed before the filler has set (top), resulting in a smaller area to sand.

Below right: After sanding, the seam is again highlighted. If all goes well, the result will be that all of the contrasting tone is removed, otherwise the process should be repeated. At this stage, the model is ready for the intakes and tail surfaces, prior to priming.

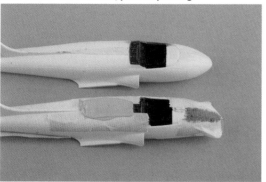 

The maritime aspect

Ship kits can pose problems of their own, especially for horizontally split hulls and larger-scale subjects, as the bigger parts can suffer from warping. A handy hint for the latter issue is to use a series of locating tabs, fashioned from styrene sheet, to keep everything aligned correctly. However, it's the former that can cause more effort, particularly for older kits designed originally as waterline models – the upper/lower hull seam can be tricky to treat without damaging other sections, especially if there's a step between the two parts. Here the solution may involve repeated filling/sanding sessions, working gradually to create a perfectly smooth surface prior to painting.

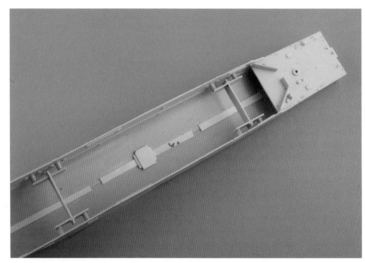

Left: Dragon's 1/350 USS *Spruance* has a long vertically split hull, which in this case suffered from warping. Strips of styrene were attached on one side to help align the underside and, in conjunction with the supplied internal cross-members, several clamps and tape, rectified the issue.

Below: The same firm's 1/700 HMS *Dragon* and *Daring* destroyers have horizontally split hulls and, despite much clamping and tape, the joins resulted in steps (bottom). The same process as used on the Jet Provost was employed here, and after two filling/sanding sessions, the seams were eliminated successfully (top).

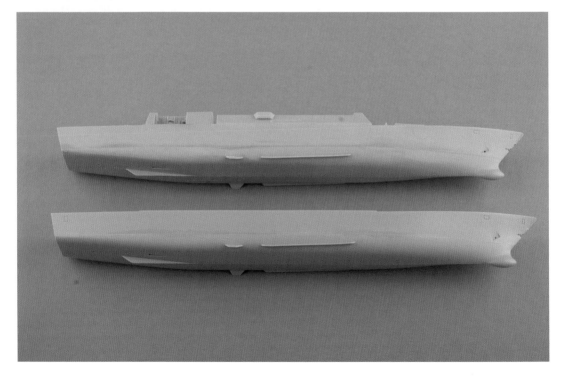

Surface marks

The method for treating blemishes is very similar to that for seams. The model's surface is given an initial sanding to highlight the area, then filled/sanded as before.

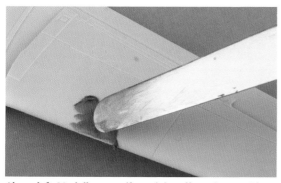 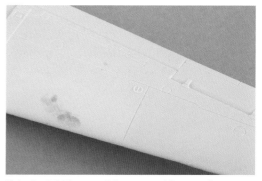

Above left: **Modellers can 'frame' the affected area with tape if desired, before applying putty with a wooden or metal spatula, which is then left to cure properly to reduce the risk of a ghost seam.**

Above right: **Once dry, the filler is sanded with increasingly fine abrasive cloths/pads until the surface is smooth. This process may need to be repeated for deeper blemishes/marks.**

Lack of lines

Modern kits represent panels using engraved lines. Once the seam has been cleaned up as desired, the chances are at least one panel line will have been reduced/removed by the sanding. You are then faced with a choice: either leave the smooth surface or attempt to reinstate the lines. There are many commercially available tools to assist in this effort, but the simplest is a sewing needle held in a pin drill. A steel rule or aftermarket scribing template can then be used, although self-adhesive DYMO tape (used in making labels) can be just as effective. The best approach is repeated light passes, running the scriber along the edge of the ruler/template/tape, as there's less chance of slipping and marking the

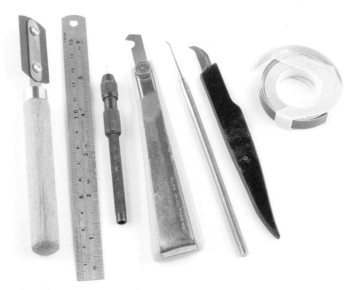

Re-scribing lines doesn't have to be a daunting process. All it takes is a scriber, a hard edge and a degree of patience. A selection of relevant tools is displayed here.

surrounding styrene – even if that happens, the amount of damage is less than if heavier pressure had been applied. Another technique is to use a small razor saw to recreate the panel lines – the remaining sections can act as a guide but, again, use only light pressure until the desired depth is achieved.

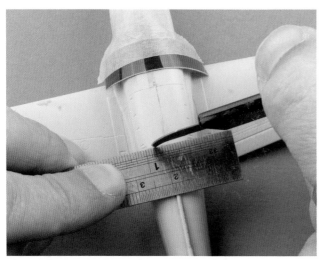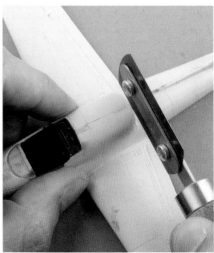

Above left: The ruler (bottom) or DYMO tape (top) is positioned along the damaged panel line and the scriber drawn along the edge in a series of light strokes.

Above right: An alternative method is to use a razor saw, but the principle is the same: align along a damaged panel line and use light passes to reinstate the detail.

Below: Once you're satisfied with your work, brushing the new panel line with liquid cement helps to remove any residual debris and smooths the edges.

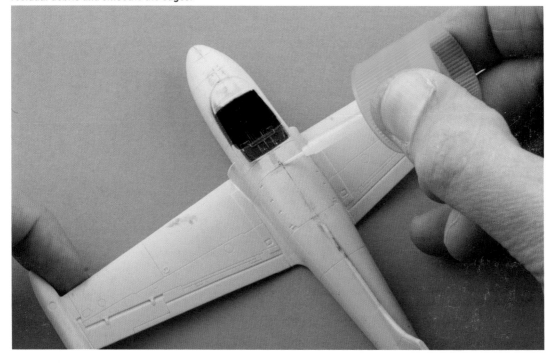

Raising repairs

Older kits may have raised panel lines. Here, you have the choice between scribing all remaining panel lines or repairing the damaged sections with stretched styrene, as shown below on a Matchbox 1/72 Provost T.I. For this, a small piece of runner is ideal. It's heated gently over a flame (a candle is ideal) and drawn out to the desired thickness – this will then be attached to the model and blended with the surface.

 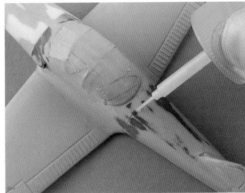

Above left: A section of runner is heated until it softens, after which it is stretched to produce a fine filament. Don't be put off if the desired thickness isn't achieved first time on the first go – it may take several attempts.

Above right: Once a suitable length has been achieved, cut it slightly too long for the repaired section and apply a small drop of liquid cement on the model in the middle of where the panel line should be.

Right: After holding the filament in place with tweezers for a few seconds, brush over the length with liquid cement and trim it to size.

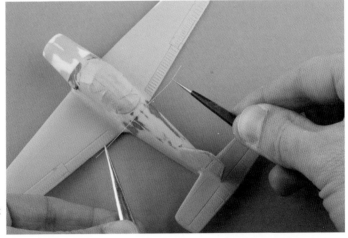

When dry, the replacement panel line should be sanded lightly to produce a slightly flattened 'top' to match the surrounding raised detail.

Chapter 6

Bring on the Brush

Basic painting tools are the respective enamel or acrylic colours, a brush, thinners and a mixing palette.

By this stage of a project, the main fuselage/hull will be completed, so the next step is to add colour. As with many aspects of the hobby, prior preparation is key, and we'll cover this before addressing how to hand paint the model, and then introduce the airbrush, to which many builders migrate. In addition to the paints, thinners and brushes, other items that will be useful are a mixing palette, low-tack tape (for masking), disposable gloves (to protect your hands) and a face mask/respirator (for use when airbrushing).

Getting ready

When preparing to add paint, it's vital to ensure the surface is clear of any dust or sanding debris, especially in the engraved panel lines. You also need to remove any grease on the plastic, which can interfere with paint adhesion. A two-step approach gives the best possible results: first wipe the surface with damp kitchen towel, then use an old toothbrush to clean the engraved detail. If necessary, the process can be repeated until the model is ready, then set it aside to dry.

The four types of paint were introduced in Chapter 1, but as a reminder these are lacquers, alcohol- and water-based acrylics and enamels, of which the last two are the most common and will be covered here. When this chapter was first considered, the aim was to use just enamels on Airfix's Jet Provost, but it was decided to include acrylics as well. The principles covered are the same for all paint types.

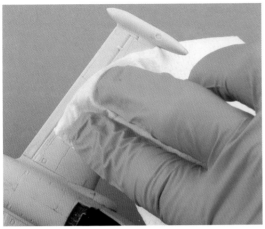 

Above left: Once any seams and/or any blemishes have been treated, the model's surface must be cleaned. This not only removes any debris, but also anything which might prevent paint adhesion.

Above right: With engraved panel lines, it's common for some sanding residue to get wedged in these thin recesses, so an old toothbrush is ideal for cleaning these areas. The model can then be wiped again with a damp tissue.

Priming

When building a basic styrene kit (ie, one that doesn't have photo-etched brass or resin components) straight from the box and not using filler, then the model can be painted once it's assembled. However, a primer (either regular paint or a specially formulated product) can help to identify seam issues (see Chapter 5) and provide a uniform surface on which to add paint. It can also help to reduce the contrast between the styrene and eventual camouflage, especially for kits with brightly coloured parts. Overall, though, the use of a primer is a personal choice.

Fresh from Chapter 5, these Airfix Jet Provosts have been cleaned and one has been primed (left), showing how this layer unifies the surface, and hides any tonal differences between the plastic and filler.

The 'hairy stick'

Often, the painting technique used by modellers when starting in the hobby is the humble paint brush, also known colloquially as the 'hairy stick', as it's simple to use and, with a little practice, can produce stunning results.

There are two primary brush types, round and flat. The former is ideal for detail and small items, while the latter is more applicable for larger areas. This type of painting is generally considered more suitable for enamels and water-based paints, due to their slower drying times compared to lacquer- and alcohol-based products. While some manufacturers state their formulations can be brushed straight from the tin/bottle, it's generally advisable to dilute the paint prior to application, as this helps it flow into the nooks and crannies and to 'self-level' before it dries. Note, some acrylic brands are branded as 'airbrush-ready' – these are pre-diluted and can be applied without any further treatment.

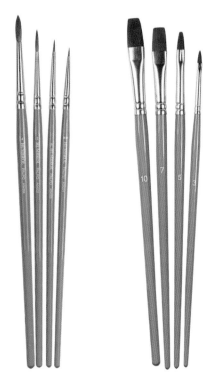

Above: Many paint manufacturers also produce their own brushes, but there are several firms that just specialise in high-quality items. While multi-item sets, such as Humbrol's rounded (left) and flat (right) packages are great for beginners, it's recommended that you should always try to buy the best you can afford (ideally, sable brushes).

Below: A quick and easy way of diluting paint is to mix it with thinners. It's best to use a company's own bespoke product, although there are now many generic types that can be used. These should be tested on a piece of scrap styrene before attempting the model, just in case the two aren't compatible.

It can be very tempting to apply a single thick layer of paint but, for the best possible results, we recommend applying at least two or more coats, building the colour density gradually. This method allows the most detail to be retained and, from a technical perspective, is very similar to how paint is applied with an airbrush.

Even with such thin paint, the difference in tone and lustre is quickly apparent. Here the wings have received their second coat, unlike the fuselage, which still exhibits a greyish tone from the underlying primer layer.

On this occasion, it took four applications of Humbrol 19 Bright Red acrylic to obtain the required density and tone on the Jet Provost, but panel lines (which could be obliterated by a thick coat) remain clearly visible.

Good housekeeping is crucial to maintaining your brushes. They should be cleaned as soon as practicable after painting has finished. This not only prevents the bristles from becoming clumped and hard, but also reduces the risk of paint build-up at the base, which can cause the brush hairs to become splayed, making it unusable.

Under pressure

An airbrush is effectively a miniature spray gun. Propellant (usually compressed air) is forced through a narrow channel and combined with paint in a mixing chamber, where it is atomised and vented through a small nozzle onto a model. There are two main categories of airbrush: single- and double-action (based on the number of movements required for paint to flow), both of which can have paint fed from above or the side (via gravity) or below (suction) and mixed internally or externally. Single-action airbrushes have just a single 'button', which is pressed to release air and paint simultaneously, while a double-action unit uses the button to allow just air through, while pulling it back (the second action) adds paint; this also enables the modeller to have greater control over paint flow.

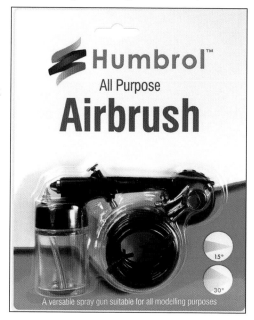

Above and right: Airbrushes come in two main configurations, single-action (Humbrol's basic suction-fed product, right) and double-action (Iwata's gravity-fed HP-CH, above).

Propellant for an airbrush can come from one of two sources: a specialised aerosol-type can or a compressor. The former can be a simple introduction to airbrushing, but will last for just a few sessions before needing to be replaced and can suffer from pressure loss as its contents become depleted. An air compressor is strongly recommended for those wanting to airbrush regularly, and basic models can be bought for less than might be expected – these have limited pressure controls, but can last for years. More expensive versions are extremely versatile (and less noisy) and come with a variety of accessories, such as moisture traps and separate pressure regulators.

Paint must be diluted before being added to the airbrush paint reservoir (even for those products labelled 'airbrush ready'), manufacturers usually have a paint thinners guide either on their website or catalogue. A basic rule of thumb is to have at least a 50:50 blend or for the resulting mixture's consistency to be close to that of milk. When airbrushing, it's important to remember that paint should be applied gradually, to ensure as smooth a finish as possible, with repeated light coats.

Airbrushes must be well maintained, otherwise they will not function properly. All products usually come with a cleaning guide, and modellers are advised to follow the process outlined in the instructions, using the same type of thinners as they used to dilute the paint. There are bespoke airbrush cleaning solutions available, but care must be taken not to mix types, as an acrylic-based product, for example, will not clean enamels or lacquers.

There are two methods of supplying propellant for an airbrush, aerosols (right) or a compressor (left). While the former is cheaper in the short term, the latter is far more economical in the long run. A very basic system is shown here, as you become more familiar with airbrushing it is worth investing in a compressor with a large (at least 2lit) reservoir as this ensures a constant pressure to the airbrush.

The airbrush should be kept at a constant distance, usually 2–3 inches (50–75mm), from the subject, with the paint applied in a series of light passes. You should always start spraying before moving the nozzle over the styrene and stop once it's clear, as this prevents any unwanted paint spatter.

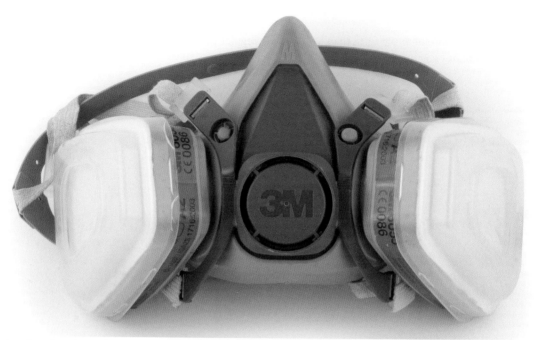

One function of an airbrush is to atomise the paint/thinners mix, which results in thousands of particles being sprayed into the air. These pose a health hazard if inhaled, so modellers should invest in a good quality respirator. It's worth spending a little extra to get a version with replaceable filters as this means just those items need replacing when they inevitably wear out. Ventilation is crucial and a spray booth is strongly recommended, as it will trap most of the paint that doesn't go on the model and vent any vapours outside.

Good and bad

Airbrushing is more of an art form than a science, so regular practice is strongly recommended. However, one or two common problems are easy to recognise.

Spidery patterns are a result of either a thinner-rich mix or the airbrush being too close to the surface – it's best to test the paint on a scrap kit or piece of styrene first.

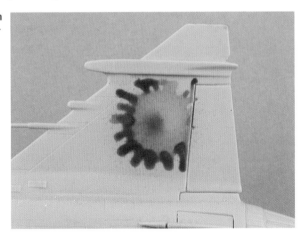

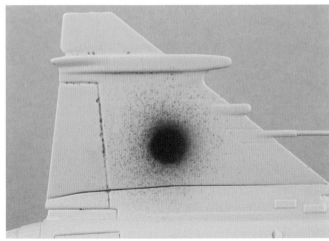

If the paint appears 'bitty' or has a speckled/grainy appearance, this generally means the paint mix hasn't been diluted sufficiently and more thinner is required.

The airbrush must be kept moving over a model's surface, otherwise the paint will build up, resulting in unsightly 'runs'. If this happens, the best treatment is to let it dry fully, then sand and respray.

Chapter 7

Marvellous Markings

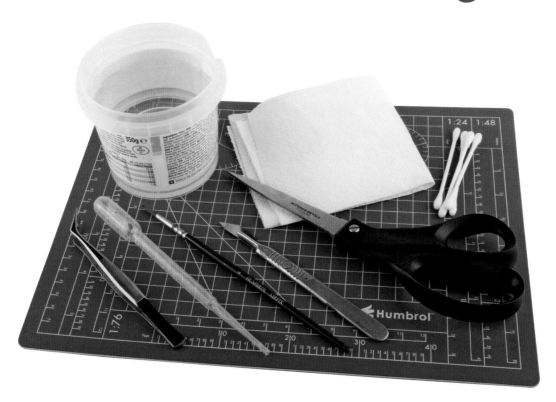

S tarting in the hobby, adding the decals (also called markings or water-slide transfers) is one of the last elements in a build project, but these can easily break – rather than make – a project if rushed.

This chapter explores the basics of getting the decals on to a model's surface (regardless of whether it's painted) and troubleshooting common issues, before introducing aftermarket products designed to aid the process. Patience is a virtue when it comes to applying transfers, as – especially if they are in older kits – they can be quite fragile. Good preparation is vital, with decals best laid on to a smooth, ideally glossy surface;

Identify the decals required for a particular scheme and separate them from any unwanted items. Here, it's vital to read the instructions thoroughly and work methodically from one end of the model to another.

Above left: A model doesn't have to be painted – wargaming or beginners' kits can often be assembled fully as the parts are moulded from pre-coloured styrene, although it's always worthwhile wiping the surface to remove any grease or dust particles.

Above right: Gloss paints are ready-made for decaling as a smooth surface is ideal; matt- or satin-painted colours may need a coat of clear gloss varnish though. These can be applied by either brush or sprayed, depending on a modeller's preference.

this can be painted, varnished or bare styrene. Just as with painting (see Chapter 6), it's advisable to wipe the model's surface with a damp tissue before you start to remove any dust or grease, as these may interfere with the decals' adhesion. Always study the instructions to determine the best approach – some require decals to be laid one on top of another, so getting the order correct is crucial.

Where to begin

In recent years, the quality of kit decals has improved markedly, with many printed by external companies, such as Microscale, Cartograf or Fantasy Printshop. The key elements of any decal are its thickness, register (whether the various colours are aligned correctly) and colour density (the better this is, the less likely any underlying shades will be visible through the markings). The thinner the decal and carrier film (the usually clear material on which the transfers are printed), the more realism will be achieved, but with the consequence that they may be more delicate to handle.

If the kit decals are of poor quality or have been damaged, then it's advisable to buy replacements, and there's an almost bewildering array of aftermarket products. As well as basic markings, there are specific sheets of airframe stencils, plus solid colours to allow modellers to make their own. Some of the best-known specialist manufacturers include Xtradecal, Microscale/ Superscale, Kits-World, Aviaeology, TwoBobs, Star Decals and Berna. Even if the exact airframe you're building isn't catered for, it's possible to combine several sets and if it's codes and/or serial numbers you're looking for, brands such as Fantasy Printshop will have what you seek, in different sizes and colours.

BASIC TOOLS

As with many aspects of modelling, having a decent set of equipment helps enormously, and all can be acquired for minimal cost. Several are common modelling tools, while others are household items, although it's always advisable to ask permission before borrowing items such as scissors. A basic set would include:

- Shallow tub
- Cutting mat
- Needle-nose tweezers
- Scissors
- Craft knife
- Paper towel and/or cotton buds
- Paint brush
- Pipette

On the model

Once you're satisfied which decals are required for a build, it's recommended they are cut from the sheet one at a time, after which they are dipped into lukewarm water for approximately 15–20 seconds. This allows sufficient time for the water to soak into the backing paper, but not enough to cause the decal to separate and float freely. Place the wetted decal on a cutting mat for a further 30 seconds or until the transfer can be moved on the backing paper. If the decal is still immobile (a good test is to try and gently move it with a wet fingertip or tweezers) then repeat the process until it lifts from the paper.

Now that it's moveable, pick up the backing paper with tweezers and transfer everything to the model, placing it as close as possible to the desired position, and then slide the decal gently on to the surface. If it appears to 'stick' to the model, then just add a drop of extra water with a brush or pipette to ease its movement. The location can then be fine-tuned with either a pair of tweezers or a cocktail stick.

Once satisfied the decal is positioned correctly, it's time to remove the excess water. A simple method is to use a piece of folded paper towel to just press on to the transfer, which forces any water, trapped air and/or decal adhesive out from underneath. This process can be repeated as required depending on the size of the transfer, working from the centre outwards to ensure the decal conforms to the surface contours. If the decal moves during this process, then it's a matter of repositioning (adding water if necessary) and then re-pressing it on to the surface.

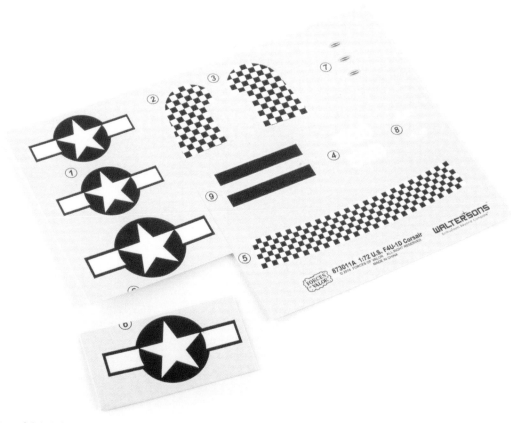

A useful tip is just to cut the minimum number of decals at a time – this helps to prevent their inadvertent loss and/or being damaged.

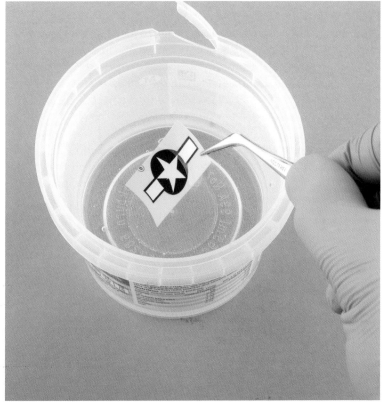

Right: Submerge the decal fully into a shallow tub of lukewarm water for approximately 15–20 seconds; this allows the backing paper to become thoroughly soaked but try not to leave it in so long that the marking becomes separated.

Below: Next, place it on the cutting mat and leave for a further 30 seconds; this gives the decal adhesive more time to soak up the water and release it from the backing sheet. A quick test to see if it's moveable is to use a fingertip or cocktail stick.

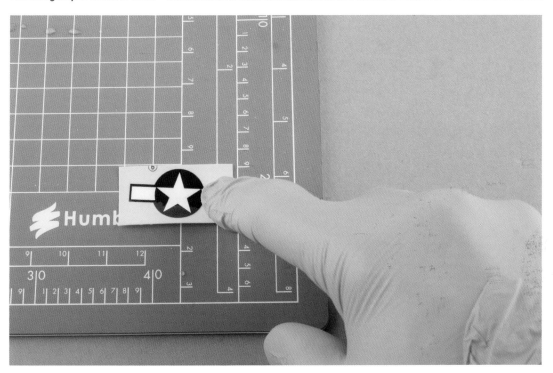

Place the decal (still on its backing sheet) on to the model and then slide the paper from underneath, so the marking rests on the painted/styrene surface.

With a paper towel, press the decal downwards on to the model to remove any excess water, adhesive and air that may be trapped underneath.

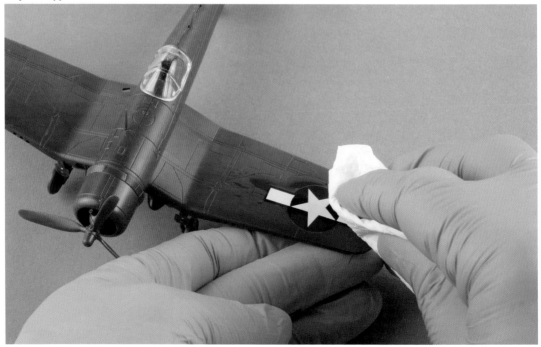

Troubleshooting

While decaling sounds simple enough, sometimes events don't go according to plan – patience and preparation should minimise the chances of something going wrong, but the most common issues are:

- Rolling/folding – There are two causes of this: either the decal has been allowed to float free of the backing paper in the water tub and it folds/rolls as its removed due to the surface tension; or the marking is so thin it lacks the 'stiffness' to be removed cleanly. For the first, it's best to return it to the water and leave it to unravel before attempting to coax it on to the backing paper. The second can be resolved in a similar fashion, or by adding a drop of water to the model's surface and then 'teasing' the folded sections with a fine brush, as this is less likely to damage the marking when compared to tweezers or a cocktail stick.
- Creases – These are caused either when the decal is positioned over raised detail or when it's intended to be placed on to a surface with compound curves, such as a nose cone, and the marking isn't flexible enough to conform. The former is best resolved by removing the raised feature carefully with a sharp knife and then attaching on top of the decal with wood/PVA glue. There are two options for the latter; either slice the decal carefully with a sharp knife and overlap the sections or use softening solutions (see *Solving problems*).
- Silvering – Arguably the most common problem, this is caused by minute air bubbles trapped under the decal and is particularly noticeable when markings are applied to matt or satin paint/varnish. Light is reflected by these tiny pockets of air, with the result the surface appears silver, hence the name. It can also occur with glossy finishes but is much less likely. The basic cure is to use a pin to prick the surface of the decal over the silvered areas, and then add water via a fine brush. Leave everything for a few minutes, then use a paper towel to remove any excess and set aside to dry. A more advanced technique involves the use of decal solutions (see *Solving problems*) but is essentially the same process.

If a decal is allowed to separate completely from the backing paper, it may fold in on itself when removed from the water. While this may appear disastrous, in most cases it can be remedied easily.

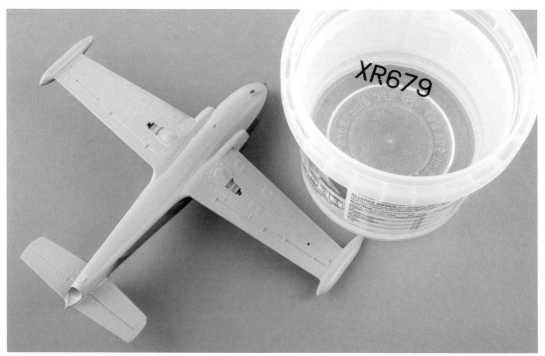

Return the decal to the water tub and allow it to unfold; if it appears reluctant to do so, manoeuvre it on to the backing paper and place it on a cutting mat, where a brush can be used to gently tease the folded sections from underneath. Care is needed not to tear the delicate decal.

If the decaling guide indicates a marking should be placed over raised detail there are two approaches – either remove the styrene and add later (as seen here) or use decal solutions.

Similarly, decals intended to cover areas with compound curves may not be flexible enough, resulting in creases as on this Fujimi 1/72 A-7B Corsair – these can be cut with a knife and the sections overlapped.

When air gets trapped under the decal, as on this Airfix Jet Provost, it results in clear sections having a silvery appearance, and is usually caused by being applied onto a matt or satin surface.

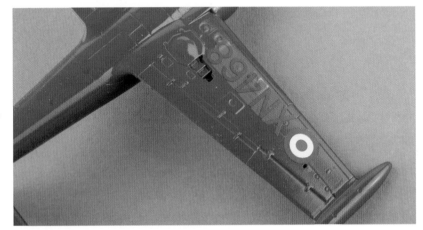

The recommended solution is to prick the decal with a pin over the silvered areas and apply either water or decal softener before removing any excess.

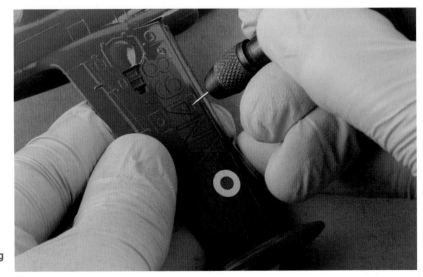

Solving problems

In recent years, the number of bespoke products aimed at easing decal application, with manufacturers releasing their own brands. These can be used with most markings, but it's always worth checking the instructions to see whether they are compatible or testing them on a spare decal. They are mildly acidic liquids, which act to soften the decal and help them to settle on to surface detail, regardless of whether its raised or engraved. The most common types utilise a two-part approach: a setting solution, which is used to 'pre-wet' the model and helps to 'draw' the decal down on to the surface, and a softener solution, which acts more aggressively to soften the transfer and 'bed down' around detail. There are various formulations of the latter product, with the strongest capable of dealing with even the thickest decal. Note, though, once the softener has been applied, the decal should not be touched, even if it starts to wrinkle (this should be expected if softener has been applied and will disappear as the decal dries) as it will tear easily. In the event of silvering, the decal is pierced with a pin as usual, but instead of water, the softener is brushed on to the decal and allowed to run into the holes. The model should then be set aside to allow everything to dry thoroughly.

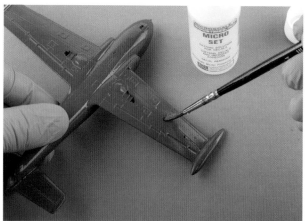

Above: There are various brands of decal solutions available, which are all designed to soften the marking and allow it to better conform to the model's surface.

Left: Setting solutions are applied prior to the decal, which is laid on top of the liquid and any excess removed as usual with a paper towel.

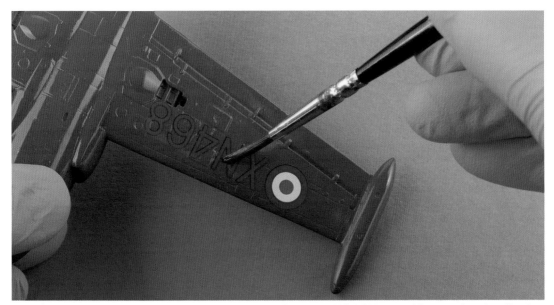

Softening solutions are designed to make the decal more flexible and 'shrink' it around features, but also allow it to stretch slightly, so it can conform with recessed detail.

Aftercare

It may take more than a single session to add all the required decals, especially if the subject is large or there are numerous airframe stencils. However, once a suitable break point has been reached, the model should then be set aside and the markings allowed to dry thoroughly, usually overnight. A dampened paper towel or cotton bud can then be used to remove any remaining adhesive residue, which also serves to prepare the surface for any subsequent decaling sessions, a varnish coat and/or weathering.

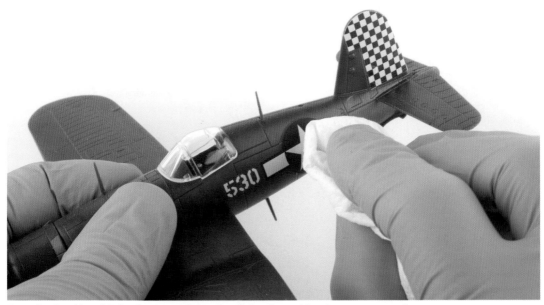

Once the decal has dried at least overnight, wipe the surface with a damp paper towel to remove any excess adhesive residue. This is recommended strongly whenever decal solutions have been used.

Chapter 8

Weather Beaten

Pick a brand, any brand – there is a huge variety of bespoke weathering products available, with many paint firms offering their own 'systems', most of which are either water- or enamel-based, although there is a growing selection of oil-based items as well.

While this chapter is concerned with weathering as one of the later stages in a build, the process and several techniques have already been introduced in Chapter 4. Here we will expand on those initial methods, hopefully break down the seemingly bewildering array of aftermarket products and offer some basic alternatives instead. As with other subjects in this series, the aim is to introduce the principles – more advanced techniques can be found either in *AMW*'s regular build features or various dedicated books. There are several rules of thumb though: practice definitely makes perfect, and 'less is more', as it's very easy to overdo the effects.

Schools of thought

Arguably, hobbyists have never had it so good when it comes to weathering, and there are two main approaches, known as the Spanish and Nordic Schools. The former was pioneered by Spanish modeller François Verlinden and results in starkly contrasting surfaces. An alternative approach was adopted by followers of the latter method, which was conceived by a group of Scandinavian modellers; this aims for a more subtle finish, based on an understanding of how real machines are affected by use, time and environment. Unsurprisingly, there is a whole spectrum of weathering between the two, and it is common to see both methods used as modellers aim for a realistic appearance.

Readers will recognise the starting point – that of preparing the surface before work begins. For weathering, it is recommended that the model is given a gloss varnish, as this makes application easier; it also seals the underlying paint layers and prevents them being affected (many products have a high thinner content, which can attack underlying layers if not protected). Looking at the subject

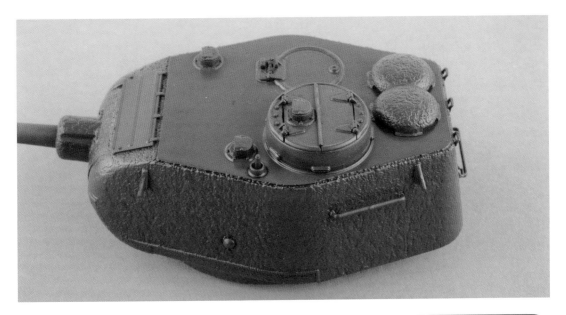

Military modellers often refer to a 'pin wash' to enhance the surface detail on vehicles, and the effect can be seen on Airfix's 1/35 T-34, with treated areas on the turret top being more prominent than the basic painted surfaces on the sides.

broadly, weathering can be sub-divided into four main areas: accentuating detail, tonal shifts, wear and tear, plus grime and mud, and these will be addressed in turn.

Accentuating detail

Highlighting features on a model's exterior is the same process as for the interior and centres on exaggerating lighting effects. Dark washes are ideal for enhancing recessed detail (such as weld beads or panel lines) and helping raised areas 'pop out', especially in combination with highlighting via dry-brushing. As noted in the *Glossary*, there are different names given for techniques applied to armour and aircraft models, but the principles are the same. Washes are also the basic element for the 'rain effect' or 'streaking' products, although the pigments used can be coarser than those found in paints.

Tonal shifts

Filters can aid modellers in several ways, either to reduce the contrast between camouflage tones (commonly referred to as 'tying together') or to add variations to monotone paint schemes. The aim is not to provide a

BASIC TOOLS

Weathering requires surprisingly little equipment, with the main constituent being a selection of paint brushes. These will include old items, which can be used with pigment application and 'scrubbing' the surface for chipping effects. Other useful implements include:

- Cocktail sticks
- Foam sponge
- Tweezers
- Paper towel and/or cotton buds
- Paint brush

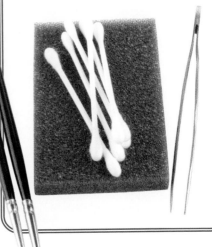

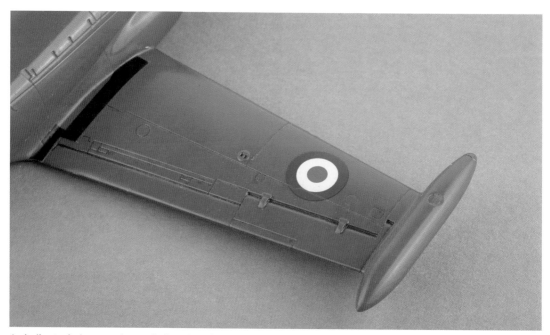

A similar technique can be applied to aircraft models, although here it's notable that the desired effects are usually more subtle – sometimes strongly contrasting tone such as black (inner wing) can be less convincing than a dark brown or grey shade (outer wing).

Dry-brushing is a simple method for applying small amounts of a lighter paint (when compared to the underlying colour) to raised detail. When used in combination with a wash, as on this engine grille, the results can be striking.

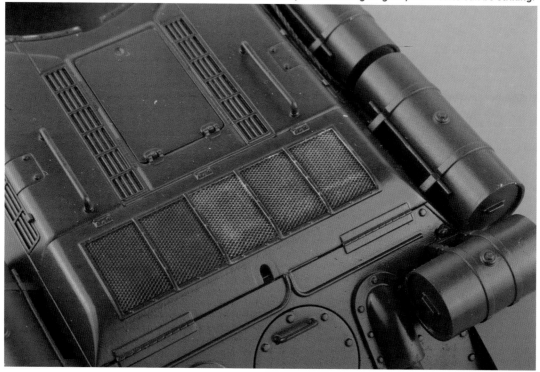

localised effect, but subtly change the overall shade by building the colour density gradually. There are many aftermarket filters available that make it much easier to achieve a given effect, with specific products for light- and dark-toned finishes. Similar results can be obtained using washes, with the fluid allowed to flow around raised and recessed detail, enhancing the appearance of both, but at the same time 'tweaking' the appearance of the surface colour.

Wear and tear

One of the most common uses of weathering is to create worn, damaged, cracked or chipped surfaces. There are many ways of achieving these effects, but some of the simplest involve painting damaged areas with a fine brush, sanding a surface until the underlying layer becomes visible, or variations on what is known as the 'hairspray technique'.

As its name implies, this involves spraying hairspray on to a painted surface (which will represent the underlying tone on the finished model) and, once it has dried, a layer of acrylic is then painted or airbrushed on top. This isn't allowed to dry fully, instead it is rubbed with a water-dampened brush, cotton bud or cocktail stick, which soaks through the upper layer and dissolves the hairspray. The result is the overlying layer flakes away in a convincing representation of abraded paint. Several companies now produce their own 'chipping fluid', which functions in the same way as the hairspray layer.

Although sun-faded surfaces can be created by careful use of pre-shading with an airbrush, another approach is to use dry-brushing to lighten the centres of panels to achieve the same result. Similarly, smoke stains from engines and soot marks from guns can be replicated in the same manner. All it takes is a degree of patience and (ideally) practice on a scrap model or piece of spare plastic beforehand until you are confident enough to work on the model itself.

One of the simplest methods of imitating abraded paint is to apply the colours directly to the model and once the top layer has dried thoroughly, sand the surface gently until the base tone visible, as seen here on this Airfix 1/48 Jaguar GR.1a.

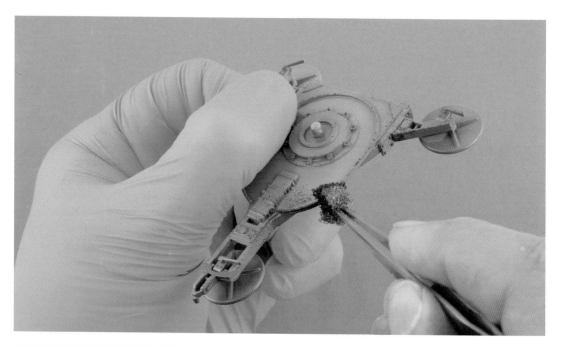

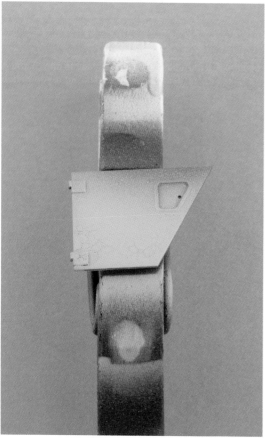

Above: Alternatively, a small piece of foam sponge can be used to add chipping – as with dry-brushing, the sponge should have almost all the paint removed, before dabbing it lightly. Here, a Das Werks 1/35 Flakvierling baseplate is being treated in this manner, with the effect applied gradually.

Left: In a variation of the hairspray technique, a chipping solution has been sprayed onto a base layer, over which a topcoat has been airbrushed – this is then left for to dry for approximately 20 minutes.

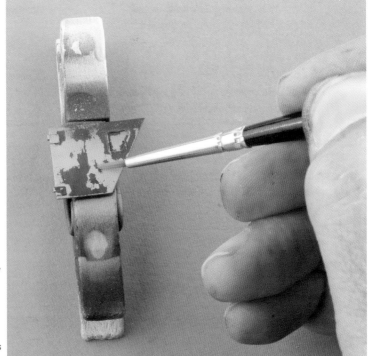

Right: The upper layer is scrubbed with a water-dampened brush to reveal the underlying tone – some modellers have adapted this method to also work with lacquers and enamels.

Below: Alternatively, and avoiding the use of any chipping or hairspray products, the underlying tone can be added on top of the camouflage, such as on this Hasegawa 1/72 A6M2-N Rufe – a fine brush is required, and the paint is added gradually to replicate worn surfaces and panel edges.

Corrosion effects, such as rust, can be approached in several ways. Here, the exhausts on a T-34 were painted dark brown, after which rust-toned pigments were added, with sooty tones applied to the burnt nozzles.

Grime and mud

As any engineer will tell you, anything mechanical will leak eventually, and the result is usually a stain or smear on the surface of a vehicle or aircraft. Look at the underside of most airframes and they are marred by streaks of oil and/or hydraulic fluid, which can transform a monotone finish into a fascinating palette of browns, reds and even greens, based on the type of fluid, all of which are forced in the direction of the airflow. Equally, when a vehicle/aircraft is left outside in the rain, over time smears will be formed on the sides – not from the rain itself, but from dust being drawn down by the water as it flows under gravity.

Replicating the effects of leaks can be achieved via oils and enamels (these are favoured by modellers as they are relatively slow-drying and can be manipulated). Dots are added to the surface at the start point, and the paint is then drawn in the direction of the airflow via a thinner-dampened brush. Soot/smoke marks can be created in a similar fashion, with the alternative being the use of pigments or paint, in combination with dry-brushing techniques. Lastly, rain marks can be rendered by adding dots of paint at the top of a panel, after which they are drawn downwards with a thinner-dampened brush. Aftermarket products are usually pre-mixed and, as with most other weathering aspects, should be built gradually until the desired effect is achieved.

A matter of cost

If you are new to the hobby, the huge array of aftermarket products available to assist with weathering can be confusing, but it's useful to remember these merely provide user-ready materials. As such, this means it is relatively easy to make your own, although getting the shades right will involve a degree

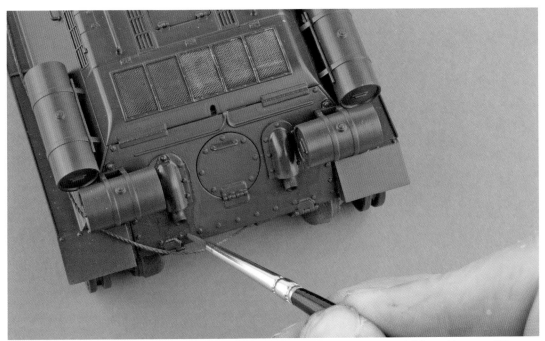

Another consequence of rusted areas is that any streaks (caused by either leaks or rain) from this area will bear those tones as well – these can be emulated via rust-toned washes, with care taken not to overdo the effect.

Smears can be created by adding drops of paint and then drawing them either downwards or in the direction of airflow – here, the undersides of Airfix's 1/48 Spitfire Mk.I have been dirtied with several oil colours.

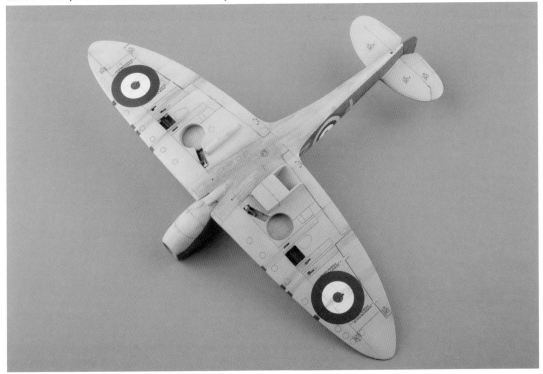

The glacis on Airfix's 1/35 T-34 has been treated with an aftermarket rain-streaking product, with the marks built up gradually. This allows for variations in the level of staining on a model, with thinners used to remove any excess, as well as enabling the streaks to be manipulated.

Pigments are ideal for creating mud effects and can be applied as desired. Here, the underside of Airfix's T-34 has received two blends: the diluted layer (right) recreates mud thrown onto the vehicle by the tracks and running gear, while a thick mix (left) is used to replicate build-ups of mud on the torsion arms.

Working from left to right, readily available materials can be used to create the majority of effects described in this chapter: diluted paint for washes, filters, streaks and stains; artists pastels for pigment work and mud; and watercolour pencils may be a cheap alternative to weathering equivalents.

of experimentation. Simpler alternatives, which can be purchased for minimal cost at arts and crafts shops are as follows:

- Washes and filters – As these are essentially diluted paint, it's just a matter of mixing a batch to your own requirements.
- Pigments – Artists pastels make for an ideal alternative, with the advantage that they can also be used like a pencil to create scratches, or ground to produce a powder that can be brushed onto the model or mixed with water to form a muddy slurry.
- Pencils – A greater degree of experimentation may be required to find a suitable brand, but artists' watercolour pencils are essentially the same as those marketed by aftermarket companies as bespoke weathering products.

Chapter 9

Varnished Truths

Varnishes have been mentioned in three previous chapters (see chapters 4, 7 and 8), so it's time to take a much closer look at these useful products.

The name is given to a colourless paint intended originally to act as a sealing/protective coat. Its use in modelling originally followed the same approach as in wood or metalworking, representing a final layer to provide an object with a matt, satin or gloss finish. However, in recent years, its applications have expanded greatly and it is now common for varnishes to be employed throughout a build project, although – as with many such aspects of the hobby – the level of usage is purely down to personal preference.

In the Klear

As with most painting products, there are four main formulations: water- and alcohol-based acrylics, enamels and lacquers, each with its own strengths and weaknesses in terms of drying time and

There are four main types of varnish available to modellers: water- and alcohol-based acrylics, enamels and lacquers. These come in standard matt, satin and gloss finishes.

Many modellers use varnishes to achieve a specific sheen on a build – here Airfix's 1/72 Spitfire PR.XIX has received an overall gloss finish.

hardness once it has cured fully (see *Pros and Cons*). Arguably, the reason that varnishes once had limited use was that they tended to 'yellow' as they aged, turning white into ochre-tinted finishes and imparting a rather unhealthy green tinge to anything blue. Thankfully, such issues are no longer prevalent, although modellers may encounter this effect with older products.

Strangely, the biggest influence on the hobby probably came from a floor polish, in the form of Johnson's Klear, a water-based acrylic 'wax' commonly used on tiles and linoleum (Note: this product has since been reformulated and rebranded as Pledge Multi-Surface Wax in Europe; in North America, it has changed from Future to Pledge Floor Gloss – even so, it is becoming increasingly hard to obtain). Not only did it provide a clear, smooth gloss finish, but it didn't yellow with age, dried quickly, could be added by brush/airbrush (including additional coats to remove blemishes) and could be cleaned with tap water. Better still, it wouldn't usually discolour when decals were applied (any that did appear that way when

PROS AND CONS

As with regular paints, the different types of varnish each have their own distinct properties, which are summarised below:

Formulation	Pros	Cons
Water-based acrylic	Fast-drying	Softer finish
Alcohol-based acrylic	Fast-drying	Softer finish
Enamel	Very hard finish	Slow-drying
Lacquer	Very fast-drying	

first applied usually dried clear subsequently), and aided adhesion while also reducing the risk of silvering (see *Marvellous Markings*). Further experimentation by modellers revealed that canopies and other transparencies could be dipped into it to produce a superb shine and would act as a fairly strong adhesive – without smearing a transparency – if flowed around a part. The icing on the cake was that any treated items wouldn't then 'fog' when cyanoacrylate (CA) adhesives were used, either to attach photo-etched components to them or nearby on the model.

Finish for all

In the past decade, there has been a virtual explosion in the number of varnishing products available to the modeller. This profusion of alternatives has been most advantageous as the original product is now hard to obtain. Many replicate the advantages of Klear (several even have the same misspelt title) but are supplied in all three types of finish. Most major paint companies now have their own proprietary versions, and this has led to a similar boom in how varnishes are used. Experimentation has shown that gloss and satin products generally appear to have the greater application outside of creating a specific finish (see *Useful properties*), which makes them an ideal starting point.

Varnishes during a build

The question of 'Where to begin?' inevitably leads to the vexed issue of 'What works with what?' This was touched on initially in Chapter 4 *Let There be Light* and is particularly true where a varnish is used as the 'filling' in a paint/weathering 'sandwich' (See *Filling the sandwich*). The last thing a modeller wants is the upper layer – whatever it may be – to react adversely with any underlying paint/varnish, so employing a diluted enamel wash over enamel paint, for example,

USEFUL PROPERTIES

The following table is best used as a guideline, as some products may act in a slightly different fashion to others – such as lacquers, which dry to a very hard surface.

Finish	Wash	Filter	Dry-brushing	Pigment
Matt	Any excess tends to stain the surrounding surface as it is absorbed.	May result in harsh results, as a matt surface will absorb the filter.	Rough surface is ideal for this form of weathering.	Rough surface means dry pigment is 'gripped' better than other surfaces.
Satin	Flows better than on a matt surface, but some staining may occur.	Recommended surface for filter application as the smooth surface ensures even coverage.	Smooth surface means there's less for the paint to 'key' against.	Good for wet/mixed pigments.
Gloss	Excellent for panel line or pin washes, as the smooth surface facilitates any capillary action.	Ideal for filters as the smooth surface ensures even coverage.	Smooth surface means there's less for the paint to 'key' against.	Good for wet/mixed pigments, especially if there is a need to 'flow' them into recesses.

Above: As with other paint products, varnishes can also be mixed to vary the final sheen subtly, such as for this eggshell finish on Airfix's 1/72 Harrier GR.9A.

Right: Products such as Johnson's Klear/Pledge Multi-Surface Wax can be used to improve transparencies, as it has a slight gap-filling capability, enabling it to 'remove' small scratches and blemishes. While this product is now increasingly hard to come by, there has been an increase in alternative products, several of which produce superior results that are far more resilient when handling clear parts. Examples include AK Interactive's Gauzy Agent range of products.

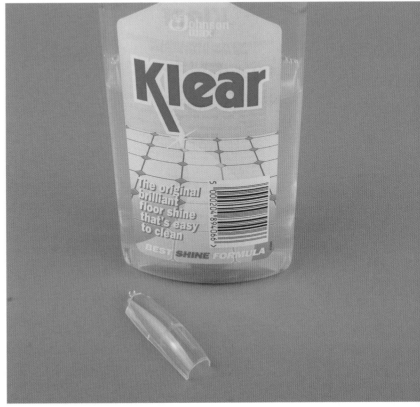

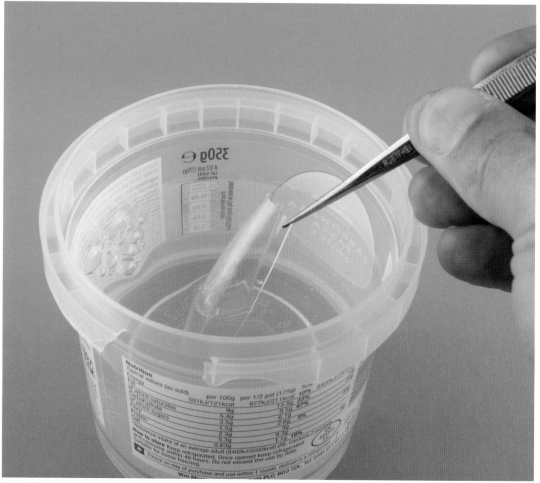

Regardless of the varnish product used, the offending item – in this case, a canopy that has had a mould seam removed – still bears minor abrasions despite the use of fine-grade abrasive/polishing pads. It can simply be immersed in the varnish and set aside to dry on a paper towel, which soaks up any excess fluid, then...

may cause damage to the underlying layer, due to the paint's high thinner content. Note that lacquer paints, especially metallic tones, are something of an anomaly, as they do not necessarily require a varnish before adding an oil-based wash (which includes enamels), although it is arguably better to be safe than sorry.

As with many aspects of the hobby, preparation is crucial. The first step is to ensure that the surface to be varnished is free of any sanding/scribing debris, dust, fluff or any other blemishes, as these will become trapped otherwise, potentially ruining the finish. It is also ideal to have specific brushes for varnishes, as this avoids the risk of any paint residue causing inadvertent contamination of this colourless layer. Otherwise it is just like adding any other shade – it is better to use several very thin coats as this reduces the potential for unsightly runs, plus these will dry more quickly than a thicker application; this is true regardless of whichever method is employed, either brush or airbrush.

Once completed, the model should be set aside to dry thoroughly. At least 24 hours will be required for slow-drying products such as enamels, and up to 12 hours for all other types of varnish, no matter how quickly they may become touch-dry.

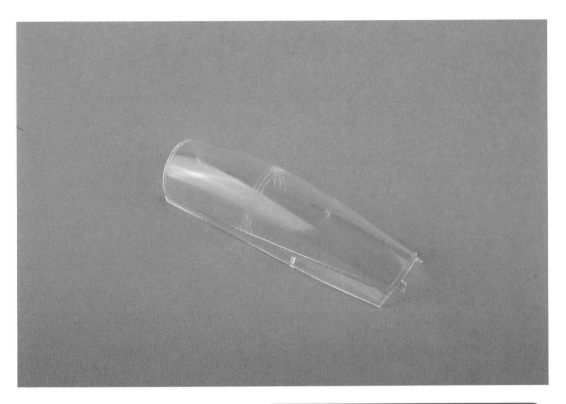

...once dry, the result is a gleaming glass-like finish, and one that won't become fogged if CA is used to attach it (or other parts) to a model.

Any alternatives?

As mentioned previously, the use of varnishes (notably gloss) during a build project is a matter of personal choice. Their application can be mitigated by the use of gloss paints or polishing the underlying layer, although a varnish may still be required for the final sheen to replicate the finish on a real aircraft/ ship/vehicle. Other methods combine varnishes with polishing the existing paint layer/layers in readiness for either decaling or weathering. What cannot be denied is that varnishes are an excellent means of protecting any previous work, especially when there is extensive handling of a model during a project, so are worth considering by any builder.

FILLING THE SANDWICH

As a final layer, there isn't a need to use a specific type of varnish, as it's just there to provide the desired sheen. However, it's advisable to use a different formula of varnish to any overlying paint/wash to minimise the chances of affecting the underlying layer. The accompanying tables offer a handy guide, although it should be stressed that it is always worth experimenting with different combinations on scrap styrene or even an old model:

Base colour	Varnish
Acrylic	Acrylic, enamel or lacquer
Enamel	Acrylic, enamel or lacquer
Lacquer	Acrylic, enamel or lacquer

Varnish	Dry-brushing/wash
Acrylic	Enamel or oil
Enamel	Acrylic or oil
Lacquer	Acrylic, enamel or oil

Left: When using Klear (or similar water-based acrylic varnishes) modellers may find it becomes opaque during decaling – this occurs due to the presence of excess amounts of water, however...

Right: ...once any excess has been removed and the model allowed to dry thoroughly, such blemishes will disappear and the original gloss finish return.

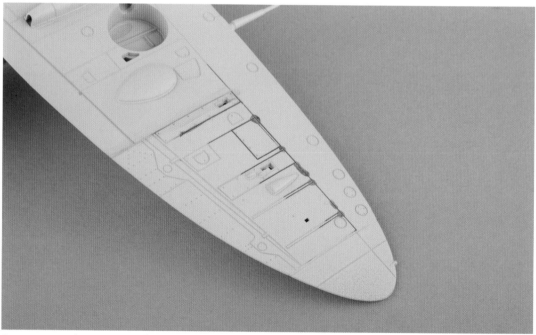

Any excess wash on a matt surface, regardless of type, will tend to stain the surface due to its inherent roughness, which causes more of the paint to be absorbed into the underlying tone. Here, the effect is tested on a Tamiya 1/48 Spitfire Mk.Vb.

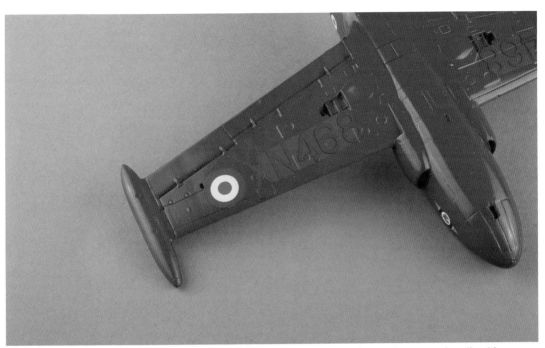

By contrast, any excess will 'pool' on a gloss/satin surface and, even when dry, can be removed easily with thinners, leaving a neatly highlighted panel line or recess, as shown on Airfix's 1/72 Jet Provost T.4.

There are consequences of using the same formulation of weathering product as varnish. The former was neatened with an acrylic thinner-dampened cloth, but this has stripped the gloss layer and paint, exposing the styrene.

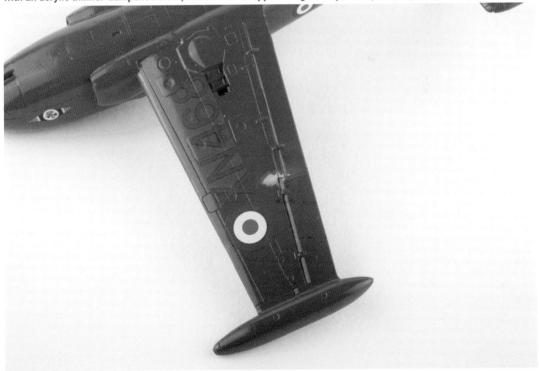

Painted parts/models should be allowed to dry thoroughly. Any surface debris must be removed before the varnish is applied – a brush is a handy tool for achieving this, as are tack-rags, which are sold at automotive stores.

If using a paint brush, it is advisable to apply the varnish (here, Humbrol's enamel gloss is used to coat the outer wing of this Spitfire) in thin layers as this reduces the risk of paint 'runs'. Any bubbles that form as the brush passes over recesses should be broken while the varnish is still wet, otherwise they will mar the finish.

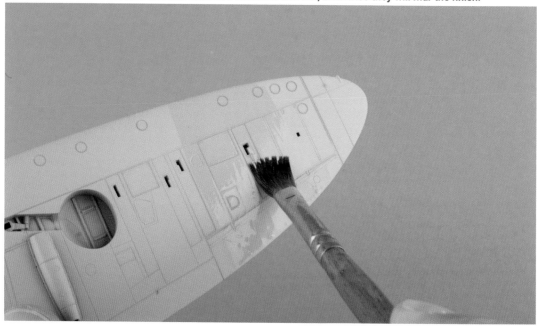

When airbrushing varnish onto a model, a similar approach is required. It is far better to spray a series of light coats than a single heavy layer.

The interior of Airfix's 1/48 P-51D Mustang was painted with matt enamels before receiving a gloss varnish in readiness for basic weathering effects.

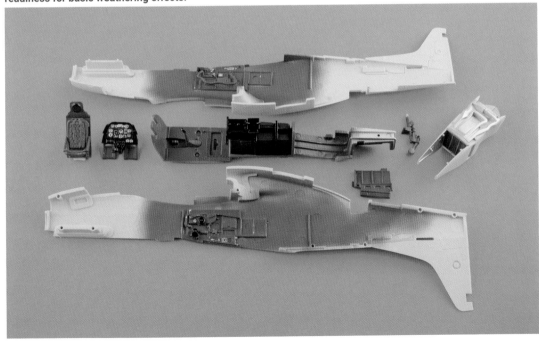

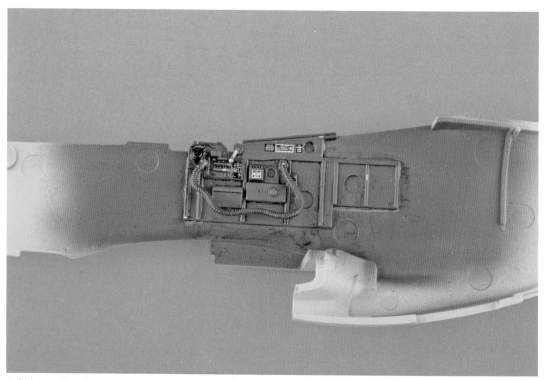

A dark-toned wash was then used to accentuate the moulded detail. Once everything had dried thoroughly, a matt varnish will be applied to provide the correct dull finish found in Mustang cockpits.

Chapter 10

Aftermarket Extras

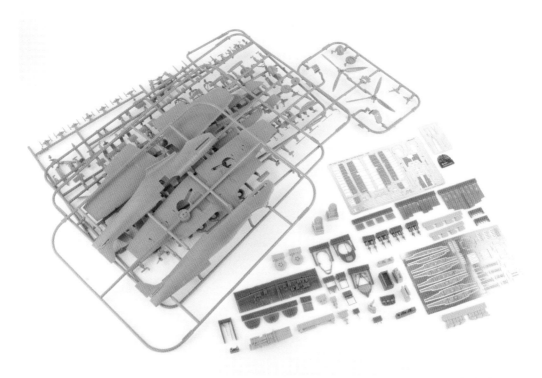

While accessories are available for most kits, some manufacturers (such as Czech firm Eduard) take it even further, releasing basic styrene products followed by a range of extras, allowing modellers to pick and choose the level of refinement.

B asic builds are often 'out of the box', but those that are intermediate and advanced generally involve extra products of varying types and a degree of scratch-building (see Chapter 11). The former are more commonly called 'aftermarket' or accessory items – although, as we'll see, some manufacturers are starting to blur these distinctions. This subject was first mentioned in Chapter 7 with regards to specific markings for a given project, so for the purposes of this chapter aftermarket will be defined as those items other than decals designed to upgrade, convert, correct, embellish (sometimes including combinations of all four) or add context to a kit.

In recent years, this aspect of the hobby has developed faster than any other, with a veritable explosion of releases from a growing number of companies – large and small – and at times the sheer volume can be overwhelming. It's now common to see a broad range of accessories emerge quickly whenever a newly tooled subject is released, by a variety of specialised companies (several of which also make their own kits), and this means modellers can engage in a 'pick and mix' approach to the level of detail/accuracy they incorporate in a project.

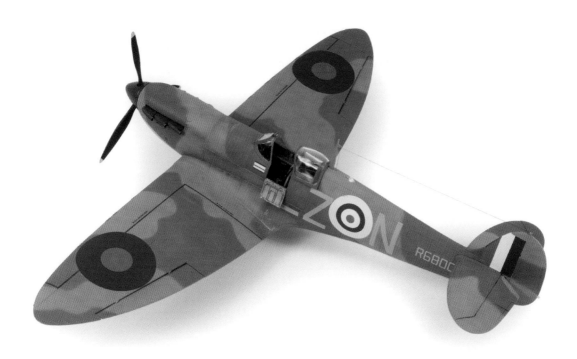

Here we can see the difference created by aftermarket products – above is a kit built 'out of the box', while the one below has received several extras, including cockpit detail and open gun bays.

However, there is a flip-side to the aftermarket equation that must be mentioned – cost. All accessories will entail an additional expenditure; depending on the age/complexity of the latter, the price of the 'add-ons' can exceed that of the original kit. Some of these items can also be far more intricate and complex (notably ship detailing sets), so it's always worth checking to see what is involved with any extras.

High fidelity

Nowadays, accessories are invariably used to add a degree of refinement – usually compensating for limitations in styrene moulding technology (regardless of the kit's age). Even conversions can offer more detail than the basic styrene, although this hasn't always been the case and older products may actually need more work to raise them to a modern standard. Note, this chapter doesn't focus on any particular model type or scale, as aftermarket products are available for any and all genres. Similarly, there is no 'age limit' – just because a kit was first released in 1960 doesn't mean there won't be accessories for it, and the recent re-packaging of vintage subjects by several manufacturers means there's a burgeoning market for extras.

Generally, there are four types of material used for aftermarket products: styrene, resin, wood and metal, although for the last of these they are split further into photo-etched, cast (white metal and bronze) and turned (on a lathe) products – each has its advantages and disadvantages (see *Different materials*). In recent years, a new type of accessory, created by 3D-printing techniques has emerged, where parts (and kits) are created by the addition of layers of thin resin or styrene until the desired shape (designed initially using computer software) has been achieved. This method is increasingly being used by resin manufacturers to create a master for subsequent casting.

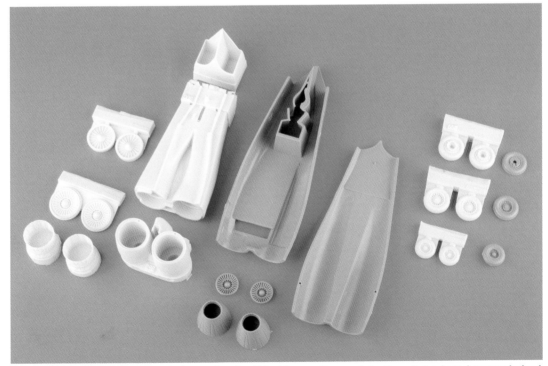

Basic kit component and improved aftermarket detail, in this case BarracudaCast's resin intake/exhaust and wheel sets for the Revell 1/48 B-1B kit, which raise the detail level considerably.

Blurred lines

It wasn't too long ago that kits were released in either styrene or resin form – items such as PE were strictly for the aftermarket companies. However, styrene extras have been commonplace for years – a Japanese consortium (Fujimi, Tamiya, Hasegawa, Aoshima and Pit-Road) all used a common runner for 1/700 ship extras that was also available as a separate product. Increasingly, though, this is changing; many armour kits now feature PE frets to cater for grilles, handles, latches and clasps, and auto releases have fabric for seatbelts, PE for fine detail, plus vinyl tubing for cables and fuel lines. Arguably, the maritime genre has seen the biggest changes, with PE now de rigueur in many kits for railings, ladders and radars. Some firms, such as Revell, have gone even further – it has added aftermarket packages to a limited range of subjects in its Platinum series that comprise hundreds of items with PE, wooden decks, turned brass barrels and even anchor chains. It's likely this will continue, with 3D components becoming increasingly common, offering modellers even more choice when it comes to levels of detail.

HANDY TIPS

While this subject isn't a true 'basic' subject, it does serve as an introduction to the myriad accessories available to the modeller. Despite this, techniques are similar to those used on model kits.

Photo-etched metal

One factor that can put people off using PE is the need to fold/bend parts before assembly, yet it doesn't necessarily need any fancy tools – at the very basic level, all that is required are sharp scissors, a Stanley knife blade, steel rule and a pair of flat-nosed pliers. That said, specially designed folding tools aren't that expensive, and make the process much easier.

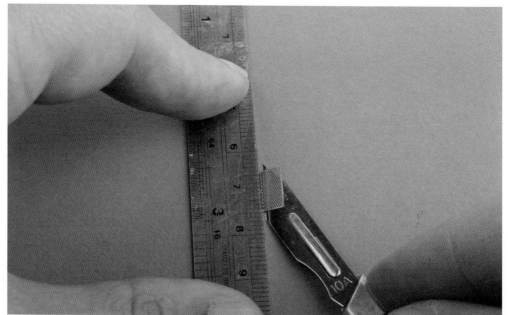

Folding a PE part is relatively easy for a simple object, although complex items can be more challenging – here the item is placed under steel rule to ensure a straight fold and the edge lifted with a knife blade.

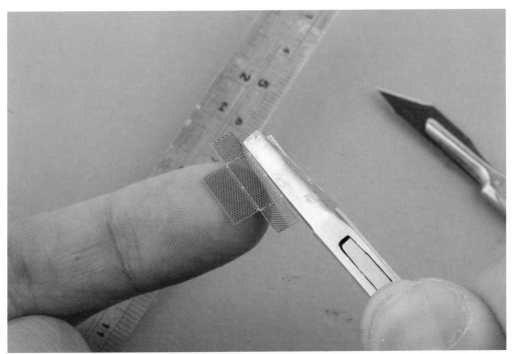

The same effect can be achieved using a pair of flat-nosed pliers, taking care to align the fold line with the edge of the jaws.

Folding tools make handling complex objects, such as this lattice tower for a ship, much easier.

Resin

Most techniques used for styrene are applicable to resin, although its more brittle nature must be considered when handling/cutting. The main concern with resin is health and safety, as the dust is harmful if inhaled, so a respirator/mask and gloves are recommended strongly.

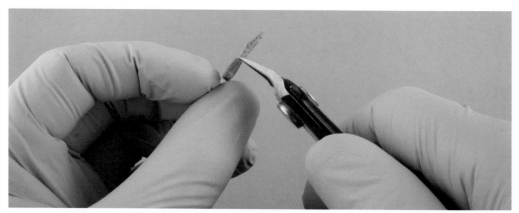

Larger components should be removed from their casting blocks using a razor saw, and smaller items, such as this Spitfire seat frame, with clippers. Immersing them in water during this process will prevent resin dust being inhaled.

One of the best ways to minimise exposure to resin dust is to sand any parts in a 'bath' of water. Modellers should ensure any worksurfaces they use when handling resin components are wiped regularly with a damp tissue/cloth to collect any stray particles.

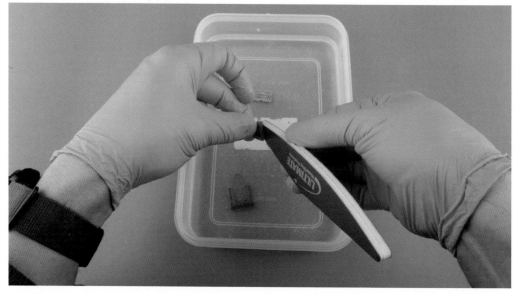

Vac-form

When removing the parts from their surrounding styrene, the best method is a three-step process: draw the outline around the component with a fine permanent marker, cut as close to this line with a sharp knife and then sand the residue until it has been removed. This last stage is best done in sections using standard abrasive paper or pads, rather than attempting to achieve it all at once.

DIFFERENT MATERIALS

Styrene
Either injection-moulded or vacuum-formed, these accessories are made from the same material as most kits. The main difference with the latter type is they must be cut from the surrounding material (instead of being separated from a runner) and then sanded until any excess has been removed. Vac-formed canopies are far thinner than their injection counterparts, making them easier to cut/pose open. Advantages include being able to focus on specific items in comparatively large numbers and on occasion other manufacturers may include them in kits to boost detail levels.

Photo-etched metal
Parts are formed on a sheet of brass, steel or a nickel alloy via chemical-etched layers. If laminated, they can be used to create convincing 3D effects, but are otherwise rather 'flat', especially when cabling is represented. One advantage of this material is it can be folded and shaped with little fuss and can be used to render extremely fine structures. Assembly will require either cyanoacrylate (CA) adhesive or the use of a soldering iron, which can make them tricky to use.

Turned metal
These products usually comprise gun barrels, antennas and other cylindrical forms, as they are created by turning and/or drilling a blank of metal in a lathe until the desired shape is achieved. The detail can be far superior to styrene, particularly for cooling jackets or other such hollow structures, as either a rod or tube can be used as the starting point. Benefits include increased structural strength, although CA is needed to mate them with styrene or resin components.

Cast metal
The most common form of cast metal accessory is white metal, which is easy to handle, being generally more robust than styrene. It's often used for individual-link tank tracks, aircraft undercarriage, ejection seats and figures – its relative softness compared with other metals means it is easy to work with but will bend if the model is heavy. Bronze items are extremely robust, although more expensive due to the casting method, and can be used for undercarriage legs and ship propellers.

Resin
When aftermarket products are described as being resin, this means they are formed from a synthetic polyurethane-based material. A 'master' shape is created, and a mould taken – liquid resin is then poured in and allowed to cure, which gives rise to the characteristic 'casting block' at the base. Advantages of resin include the ability to render much finer detail than with styrene, such as cockpit consoles, engine cooling vanes or roughened armour surfaces. However, the material is more brittle than styrene, and larger resin items can suffer from warping, although this can be resolved by immersing them in hot water and bending them back to the correct shape.

Wood
Typically balsa or bass, parts are shaped by either a machine cutter or, increasingly, by laser, and the resulting components can be quite intricate. Preparation time is minimal, although modellers will need to use a water-based PVA or epoxy adhesive, as wood will absorb other glues without sticking.

The advent of 3D printing is set to revolutionise the aftermarket industry – as seen here, a jet nozzle that previously required multiple components can be rendered as one or two pieces, yet without compromising on detail.

Chapter 11
Scratch-building Starters

While other aspects of the hobby may be regarded as being more challenging, few are regarded as enigmatic as scratch-building. However, if all the mystery is stripped away, all it boils down to is the ability to cut a series of basic shapes and then build them into an object, regardless of whether it's large or small – the complexity of the work is purely a personal decision. So, for those modellers wondering where the cauldron or magic wand is involved – don't worry, they're not needed! This set of techniques has myriad uses, whether it's adding detail/refinement, repairing a broken part or converting a kit. Again, while it might seem daunting, it's often surprising just how easily a complex object can be broken down into a series of simpler shapes. It's also great for those modellers working to a budget and so can't afford the latest accessories – indeed, sometimes the effects achieved can equal those from resin or photo-etched metal.

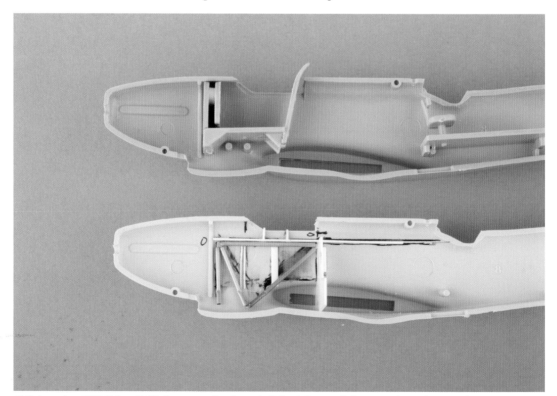

Airfix's ageing 1/72 Fairey Battle has a very basic cockpit (top), but modellers wanting to improve its appearance can fashion the innards from styrene sheet and strip, while the interior framework is created via Albion Alloys' brass tube and Connecto multi-joint adapters (bottom).

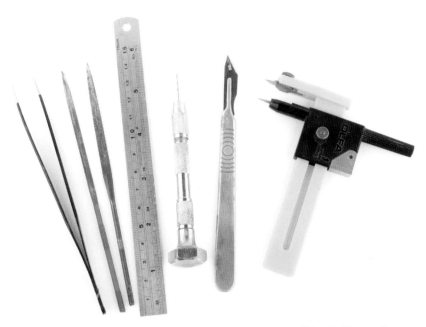

Here are the most common tools used when scratch-building, most of which will be familiar, as they are part of a modellers' regular toolkit.

Commercially available products offer a whole host of possibilities, with varying widths/thicknesses/diameters of product in either styrene or metal.

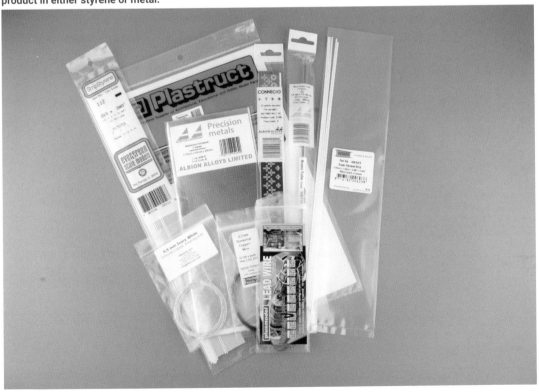

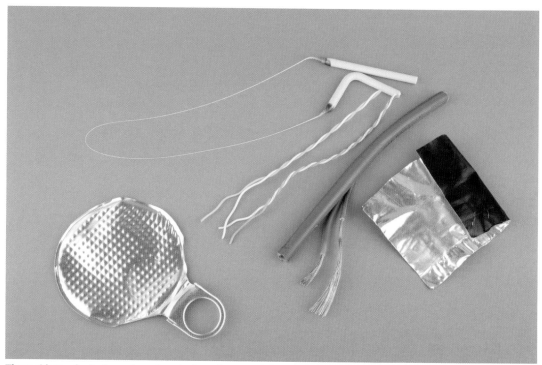

That said, you don't always have to splash out for materials – heat-stretched styrene runners have a huge range of applications, while everyday items, such as electrical wire, wine bottle wrapping and even coffee jar seals, can be equally useful.

Where to begin?

The basic toolset is readily familiar to modellers, comprising a pencil/pen, steel ruler, sharp craft knife, files, abrasive paper/pads, pin vice, magnifier, tweezers (for those small items), compass cutter and a selection of references. With these, almost any shape can be produced.

When it comes to the materials used, you can opt for either commercial or homemade items and both can be equally effective. Brands such as Maquette (www.albionhobbies.com), Plastruct (www.plastruct.com) and Evergreen (www.evergreenscalemodels.com) are among the most commonly known, and these supply a range of plastic sheet, strip, rod and tube suitable for the majority of projects. Several kit/accessory manufacturers, notably Plus Model (www.plusmodel.cz), have released their own plastic card sheets and items such as lead and copper wire, while the selection of metal sheet, rod and tube has expanded greatly in recent years with the advent of Albion Alloys (www.albionhobbies.com). For those on a budget though, it's worth remembering that many household and hobby items can also be pressed into service, from electric or computer cable, cocktail sticks, wine bottle wrappings, coffee tins (including the sealing 'plate') and even kit runners.

Getting started

Once you've gathered the relevant materials and tools, it's worth double-checking just what work is to be done – if there's a golden rule for scratch-building, it's invariably 'measure at least twice and only then cut'. Repairs are often the simplest form of scratch-building; replacing a specific section of a broken item for instance (see *Repairs*), or making a part (see *Making replicas*) to replace one that's been lost (although invariably it will be found once a new one has been crafted). The first step is then

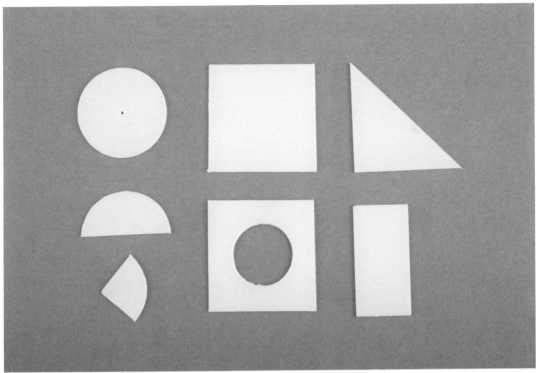

No matter how complicated a structure, it's often surprising just how easy it is to break it down into the basic shapes shown.

to determine the basic shapes involved and cut them to size – they can then be mated and/or laminated to create the correct dimensions. If the joins aren't perfect, then they can be treated with filler/abrasive pads/paper as per any other styrene part.

The same is true if short-shot parts are encountered; here, the usual injection moulding process hasn't worked properly and components will be deformed to a lesser or greater degree. While replacement can be ordered from the manufacturer, it's often just as easy to rebuild the missing elements from styrene (see *Shot to pieces*) and then trim/sand them to the correct shape.

One material often overlooked in favour of commercial products is the kit's styrene runners, which can be used as stock for scratch-building or heated and then stretched to create various thin diameters. The applications are numerous, from antenna wires, pitots and bracing struts to cockpit switches, cabling or even to repair raised panel lines on older models (see Chapter 5).

Improved quality

When it comes to adding detail to a kit, scratch-building really comes in to its own. Whether it's the simplest of framework representations to completely new compartments, all are possible. As fitting into the confines of an existing fuselage/hull can be challenging, more advanced tools may make these efforts easier, such as hobby profile gauges (for curved/complex shapes), calipers (for precise measurement) and a punch-and-die set for small diameter circles and/or holes. With practice, the scope of projects can be expanded, from super-detailing an interior or exterior to building entire models from styrene sheet – as ever, references will be crucial for such endeavours.

While plastic card is viable for most scratch-built items, occasionally a more robust substance is required, and sheets of very thin aluminium are available for those wanting to replicate convincing damage to metal object, such as mudguards or track skirts. These have the advantage of being more malleable than plastic without breaking, while also holding a shape better.

Once you've mastered these basic skills, the world's your scratch-building oyster!

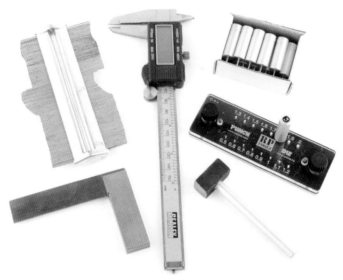

Once you've acquainted yourself with the basic techniques, the following more specialised tools may find their way into the hobby room: calipers, profile gauges and a punch-and-die set.

Using a profile gauge is relatively simple; here it is used to create a bulkhead for Airfix's 1/72 Fairey Battle by pressing it against the fuselage's interior contours.

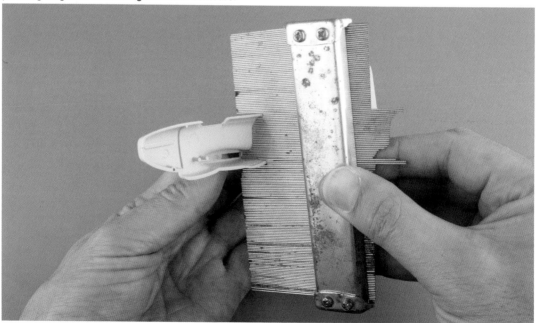

The shape is then transferred to a sheet of plastic card and cut out, ready to be fitted into the fuselage.

The inner surfaces of the Battle fuselage are plain, so lengths of styrene strip are employed to recreate internal structures – the tubular framework employs brass tube, linked by Connecto joints.

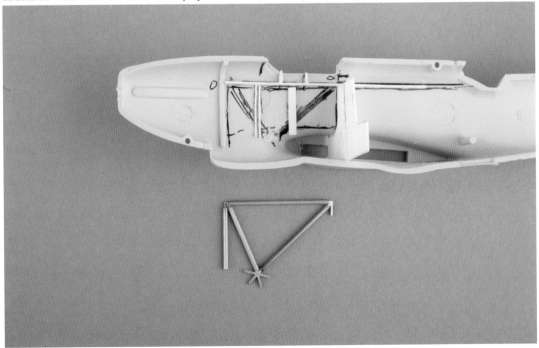

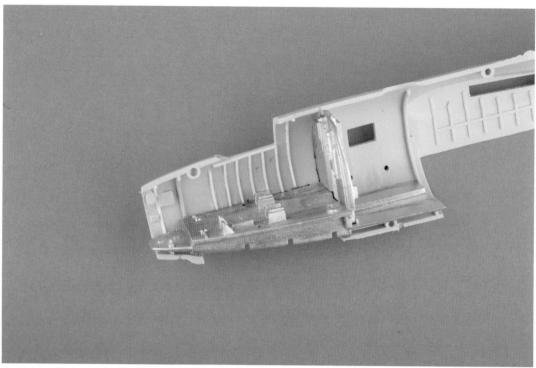

Scratch-building can also help to incorporate aftermarket accessories – here a Scale Aircraft Conversions (www. scaleaircraftconversions.com) white metal undercarriage bay/cockpit floor designed for the Hasegawa kit has been added to prevent the Airfix 1/72 B-26 Marauder being a tail-sitter – framework is replicated using styrene strip.

The seat in Airfix's Battle is very basic, so after checking references, a replacement was scratch-built. First the 'bucket' pad was created, after which the round-topped back, seat cushion and side panels were added. Once the basic form has been constructed, it can be treated as any other part, with edges shaped by sanding or filing, after which extra refinement, such as seatbelts, can be added if desired.

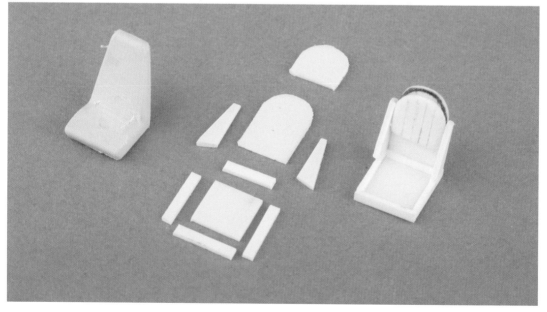

Metal sheet, such as this 30-thou (0.75mm) aluminium from Albion Hobbies, can be used to replicate items such as much guards, enabling a modeller to recreate convincing dents and tears in the material – effects that would be challenging to make in styrene.

REPAIRS

Broken parts can be the bane of a build project, with rods often the most difficult to repair as the gluing surfaces are small. Here, a missile rail from Hasegawa's 1/72 F-106 has suffered while being removed from the runner.

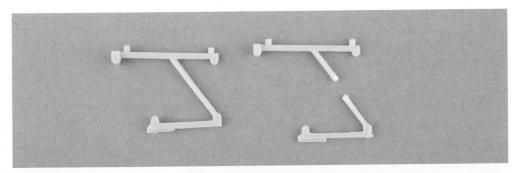

Above: While a spot of glue could repair the damage, it's arguably better to replace the broken section with a new length of rod – either metal or styrene would be suitable, with locating holes drilled into the part to accept the new component.

Right: Once inserted, the result is a repaired missile rail that is potentially much stronger than if the broken ends were just re-attached, with the advantage there's no risk of a discontinuity along its length.

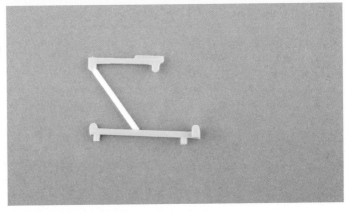

MAKING REPLICAS

Another issue can be when a part is lost. Here a control column for an Airfix 1/72 Spitfire Mk.Ia has been 'misplaced'; two methods will be highlighted: using commercial products plus those from the hobby room.

Above: The first step is to determine the basic shapes. Thankfully, this part has relatively simple components, a rectangular 'stick', circular 'handle' and (for those adding fine detail) cable runs on both sides plus a small circular firing button.

Right: Recreating these with commercial products is easier; just select appropriately sized strip and coated wire for the handle. Using the kit runner, though, means scraping a shape from a small section, plus a loop of electrical wire for the top.

Below: Once assembled, both form perfectly useable replacements although a modeller's 'Murphy's Law' may then apply, whereby the original part will be found once the replacement has been fashioned, painted and attached to the model!

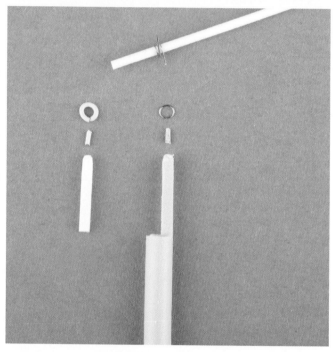

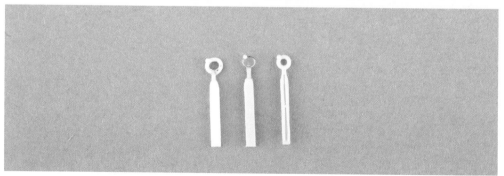

SHOT TO PIECES

Although less of a problem with modern kits, occasionally parts can be 'short shot', as in the styrene hasn't filled a mould fully, which results in a deformed component.

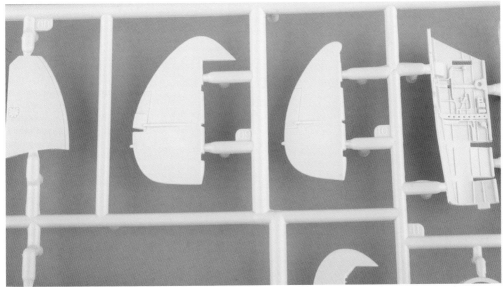

Here the rudder on an Airfix 1/48 Spitfire Mk.XIV has suffered from this issue (right), when compared to a correctly shaped item (left).

The proper shape is recreated with sections of plastic card, which are then trimmed and sanded until they match the correct profile.

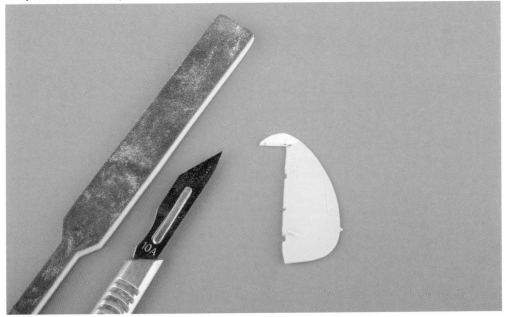

Chapter 12

Looking it Up

As with many aspects of our hobby, the past few years have seen an explosion in the amount of reference material available, almost to the point that it can be a cause of bewilderment as to where to start.

When it comes to making a model as accurate as possible, or seeking out an elusive or eye-catching scheme, then published information, regardless of whether it comes in soft or hardcopy, is invaluable. Photographs are an excellent means of spotting mistakes or oversights made by kit manufacturers and adding extra detail, plus books can also provide inspiration regarding alternative colour schemes, weathering and either internal or exterior detail.

Generally, it used to be that reference products were split into two categories: an examination or analysis of real subjects or guides to modelling. Recently though, there have been more publications that blur the lines between the two, such as Valiant Wings' Airframe & Miniature books, which provide a wealth of inspirational profiles. Equally, some of the better kit and aftermarket decal sheets are often good references in their own right, such as Eduard's ProfiPACK offerings and markings by Aviaeology and Fündekals but these can only go so far.

Eureka!

Many modellers will confess to spending hours delving into books, often purely to seek inspiration. Whether it's because the markings in the kit are not particularly exciting, or just not to their taste, an evening studying a subject will almost always offer up a photograph, illustration or text passage that will help with the way forward. This is usually followed by a hunt through mail order retailers' websites for a desired decal sheet!

Mostly, the markings you seek will be available for the subject you desire – for those rare subjects not catered for directly, there are plenty of generic serials/insignia sets to create a specific machine. Some books, such as those in Osprey's Aircraft of the Aces or Combat Aircraft series, are excellent if you wish to build on a theme. For example, US 8th Air Force fighters of World War Two is a hugely popular and well-covered arena, and, accordingly, books on P-51 and P-47 aces are available.

Nooks and crannies

When making any model, it's always good to have references to hand, as they are invaluable for the painting of cockpits, wheel wells, weapons and the airframe itself. While there used to be just a few publishers catering to such aspects, there is now a huge variety of sources with a combination of generalist and specialised products. Even niche subjects are covered extensively nowadays: publishers such as Desert Eagle and Sabot cater for fans of Israeli and US armour, respectively, and are often regarded as the 'go-to' references on those subjects.

When it comes to World War Two military equipment, the Panzerwrecks and Nuts & Bolts families of walk-around-style books are hard to beat, exploring each subject in great depth and offering wartime photos and colour profiles/artwork. If it's purely close-up detail photography of aircraft you seek, then arguably Duke Hawkins and DACO are the most applicable for serious detail hounds. These ranges are small, but cover every aspect of an airframe, including the weapons and sensors.

Modellers in mind

Inevitably, there are many books dealing with the subject of modelling itself – indeed, this has almost become a mini-industry in its own right, with many kit and accessories companies releasing one or more of their own 'how-to' guides, invariably orientated to the use of their own products. Many assume no prior knowledge, but even those aimed for the more skilled builder can act as inspiration for those new to the hobby. Also, a great number of titles solely examine the building of a particular type, or family of aircraft, tanks or ships – figures, fantasy, sci-fi and real space subjects are also popular. These can be wonderful for the beginner but can also serve the more experienced modeller. After all, we're never too old to learn.

If you'd like to enter the world of maritime modelling, Pen & Sword imprint Seaforth Publishing offers handy builders' guides, which list past and present kits and contain artwork, detail photos of the real thing and gallery sections. Recent examples include Admiral Hipper-class cruisers and Essex-class aircraft carriers.

Some of the most useful books in recent years are those that offer text and digital colour illustrations, but also decals for the machines depicted. Polish publisher Kagero led the way with this format and it now has a large range, covering everything from the Battle of Britain and the Spitfire Mk.VIII to specific titles such as the *German Panzer Arm in Poland* and *Fighters over Japan*. The decals are of excellent quality and they, along with the books themselves, enable the modeller to build on a theme, which can be great fun while also expanding a modeller's knowledge on a subject.

Information overload

The sheer weight of reference material can be enough to make the head spin, but once you identify your requirements a wealth of information can quickly be at the fingertips, whether it's through printed matter or a computer. Do not forget that airshows can also be a brilliant way to get to know aircraft (and military vehicle shows and naval 'open days' offer similar benefits for fans of military and maritime models). One can usually get fairly close to the subject and the crews will often be happy to answer questions about what's loaded on the aircraft. Renovated vehicle owners are generally happy to allow picture-taking too, so don't forget your camera!

Web 'intelligence'

The internet is packed with reference material and most subjects can be 'Googled' to good effect, while dedicated modelling sites offer handy articles and photographic 'walk-arounds'. As with all online sources, it's always worth double-checking the validity of the information – especially profiles – as not all are accurate and it's useful to find a photograph of the particular subject just to make sure. If it's more information on a given kit that you're after, then the Scalemates modelling database (www.scalemates.com) is an ideal starting point, as it includes links to 'out of the box' and build reviews of many kits and accessories. One common thread among modelling sites is that they generally all have forums, and these can be an excellent source of information. What may seem like a basic question to the masses will often solicit friendly and helpful replies.

Glossary

Ancillaries

This is something of a 'catch-all' for those items (such as figures, weapons and equipment), that add to a model's appearance but otherwise don't change the level of refinement. Modellers can choose between individual items, usually presented in resin and/or PE or sets, which are often styrene.

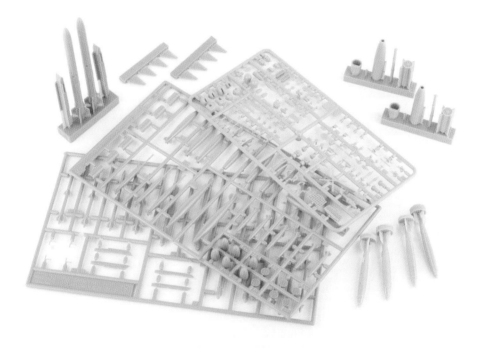

Often, ancillary items either aren't included in a kit, or if present are in limited numbers, so aftermarket items can transform the appearance of a model – a selection of aircraft and ship extras are shown here.

Chipping

The name given to reproducing the appearance of abraded paint surfaces, it can be replicated by painting/sponging the surface or utilising hairspray as a dissolvable layer (between the base and top coats of paint) to reveal the underlying shade.

Conversions

Some subjects exist in multiple variants in real life, but the available kits may concentrate on just one or a few of these and a conversion set allows the modeller to change the version of a given subject. These alterations may be subtle (involving the moving of panels or addition of equipment), or they may be

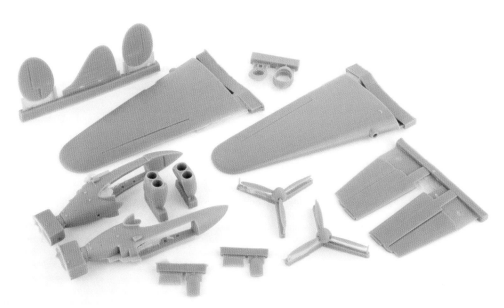

Avro's Lancaster is a very popular subject in 1/72 scale, but there hasn't been a mainstream kit of its predecessor, the twin-engined Manchester – conversions, such as Blackbird's resin set, enable this variant to be built.

major – whereby complete or partial replacement hulls/airframes are supplied. Often, older sets tend to be rather simplistic, but modern conversions can be highly intricate, and occasionally contain more components than the original kit.

Corrections
On occasion a kit is released that inadvertently contains errors, either due to a mistake in research or limitations in moulding techniques. Correction sets seek to address these issues and increase the overall accuracy of a model – they can be a combination of upgrade and conversion depending on the size of the original error.

Cyanoacrylate
Commonly abbreviated to CA and also known as superglue, this is a fast-drying adhesive that can bond dissimilar materials. It requires careful use as it readily bonds skin, as well as a ventilated room as the fumes can be quite strong, depending on the brand. When mixed with baking powder, it forms a quick-drying and very hard filler. Note that although the bond formed by CA is strong in terms of holding an object in place, it doesn't tolerate shearing stresses (those parallel to the mating surfaces) and can appear quite brittle in such cases.

Decals
Commonly called transfers or markings, the most common types are designed to be soaked in water prior to application. However, there are also 'dry' versions, which are placed against a model's surface and transferred by burnishing them with a hard-tipped object, such as a ballpoint pen or rounded wooden dowel.

Dioramas/Vignettes
Whenever a model is set into a scene (with or without figures) much of the surrounding equipment, buildings, vegetation and, on occasions, the base itself can be purchased individually

as aftermarket items. This is arguably an industry all its own, with some companies providing just forms of vegetation, for example, while others specialise in buildings, fences, and walls. This theme has huge cross-over with wargaming and railway modelling and it is common to see items developed for one side of the hobby used in one or more of the others, just as with items such as weathering products.

Dry-brushing

This is a process using an almost paint-free brush to add small amounts of lighter-toned paint selectively to raised detail, usually on the edges or upper surfaces to simulate higher reflection from these areas. Pigments can also be applied via this method, with the fine particles worked into the detail and surface texture.

Ejector pin marks

These are the small raised or sunken circular marks on styrene that are a result of ejector pins, which are used to free the runners from the moulds. Most are usually positioned in unimportant locations, but occasionally they are in areas such as the cockpit or undercarriage bays and will need removing for a smooth surface.

Filler

Any self-drying product used to rectify gaps and/or blemishes can be described as a filler, but here this definition is limited to pre-prepared putty products. It's recommended that protective gloves are worn when working with fillers, and if any gets on the skin it should be washed off immediately. There are essentially three main types:

- **Polyurethane/acrylic:** Characterised by fine pigment, quick-drying properties and low odour, these can be manipulated with water-dampened cotton buds, and any excess removed with a kitchen towel. They are ideal for applying filler into awkward places, but can suffer from shrinkage.
- **Lacquer/toluene:** The most common type available, these have relatively fast drying times, but must be used in a well–ventilated room due to their pungent vapours.

Flash

This is the excessive amount of styrene that has seeped between the mould halves. It's usually very thin and easy to remove, but this can be a time-consuming task on smaller components or where it has filled gaps in parts.

'Ghost' seams

These occur when the filler hasn't cured fully before sanding and/or painting and continues to shrink, revealing the location of the original blemish. Although not as obvious as an untreated join line, it can be disconcerting to discover one of these either right at the end of a build or once the model is on display. Other than undertaking remedial repairs, the key is to allow the filler to dry properly.

Mould seams/seam lines

These are the raised lines, usually running longitudinally along part edges, which correspond to the join between the mould halves and are formed during the styrene injection process. These can vary in appearance from a very fine raised line to flash (see below) or even a step in the plastic if the moulds are misaligned.

Mould stubs

Similar to the ejector pin marks, these are the cylindrical 'bits' attached to parts and are increasingly common as manufacturers seek to include greater detail on each component. They are there to provide overflow of the injected styrene and allow for an equalisation of the pressure; they also serve as additional ejector pin positions, aiding removal of very fine components from the moulds.

Runner

Also known colloquially (but somewhat erroneously) as sprues, these are the styrene frames which carry the parts. The vast majority are formed by injecting styrene into a two-piece mould, which leaves a slight seam where the two halves join. More advanced techniques involve a process known as 'slide moulding'. This process involves several precision-machined tools that slide into position and produce much finer detail and fewer seams.

Scale effect

The actual colours used to paint real vehicles, aircraft and ships can appear too dark on a model. An ideal example of this is black – often a very dark grey can be more convincing in a cockpit than true black. Scale effect can be achieved by lightening the base colour slightly, although this is often a personal choice, as what appears correct to one modeller will seem wrong to another. One advantage is that surfaces treated in this manner are often easier to modify with shadows/highlights.

Two-part epoxy putty/clay

These come as two separate components, usually with a consistency similar to Plasticine. These must be mixed thoroughly, after which they start to cure – this process is slow (some take up to 24 hours), enabling them to be used for large repairs or sculpting.

Upgrades

These are the most common types of accessories and include update/detail-up sets, which are designed to increase the level of refinement, by revealing internal fittings or more refined features. For example, an aircraft kit may use decals to represent an instrument panel, but the aftermarket set may use photo-etched metal or resin to allow much smaller features to be incorporated.

Wash

Usually formed from a diluted paint mix that's darker than the interior colour, this is applied with a broad brush – the fluid will gather via capillary action around raised items, accentuating a shadow effect at the base, exaggerating their 'height'. The most basic form comprises just paint and the corresponding thinners, although there are now a multitude of brands offering pre-mixed products for a whole variety of tones. Note, while a filter is similar to a wash, the former is intended to create tonal variation on surfaces, not to highlight detail. Other forms of wash are commonly employed on the exterior of vehicles/aircraft. These are:

- **Pin wash:** The name is derived from the use of a fine paint brush to exaggerate small features, such as weld beads, rivets and bolt heads on the exterior of armoured vehicles
- **Panel line wash:** As the name suggests, this is a wash applied to the engraved lines on an aircraft's exterior. It's a very common addition to models, even if this effect is not actually visible on the full-size machines.

Other books you might like:

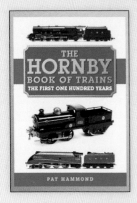

Historic Military Aircraft
Series, Vol. 5

Military Vehicles and
Artillery Series, Vol. 1

Air Forces Series, Vol. 4

For our full range of titles please visit:
shop.keypublishing.com/books